D1106186

RESEARCH LIBRARIANSHIP

RESEARCH
LIBRARIANSHIP

ESSAYS IN HONOR OF
ROBERT B. DOWNS

EDITED BY JERROLD ORNE

R. R. BOWKER COMPANY   New York & London, 1971

Published by R. R. Bowker Co. (A Xerox Company)
1180 Avenue of the Americas, New York, N.Y. 10036

International Standard Book Number: 0-8352-0487-1
Library of Congress Catalog Card Number: 78-163902

Printed and bound in the United States of America.

CONTENTS

v

PREFACE

To have a role in a work dedicated to Robert B. Downs is, in my view, an honor in itself. There can be no doubt that the contributors to this volume have written their essays with this thought in mind, for each of them carries a heavy burden of professional activities. The work of putting together this book has been done in order to express the respect and affection we all feel for Robert B. Downs.

In other times, when the speed of change in our world was less hectic, and even more now, a time for pause is welcome. A landmark occasion is a good time for this, and the end of a brilliant career is just such an occasion. Because of his honored place in our profession, the usual pattern of festschriften just didn't seem adequate for the retirement of Robert B. Downs. Our profession has reached a critical stage in a broad range of its primary fields, and it is precisely in those fields, represented in this volume, that Downs was most active and strongly influenced our current practice. Now he must pass the leadership to other hands; some of those are found here.

The essays gathered here constitute, in a sense, the distilled essence of our experience and understanding in vital areas of librarianship today. Those leaders of the profession nominated to record their views were carefully chosen for their special competence in their respective fields. Their subjects were chosen to comprise a wide spectrum of current issues, including many for which new solutions must now be found. It is timely and proper that we should now pause, read, and reflect, before we move on. This book is not intended to be definitive or terminal; it is designed to help assure a comprehensive base for future planning. At no time in the history of research libraries has the building of library collections been more contentious. Seldom has the goal of building great libraries been questioned; now this too requires reconsideration. New concepts of library use and service compel new thinking. The true measure and functions of the bibliographical record and regional or national availability are also now being critically reviewed, with change clearly the only wholly predictable outcome. Library cooperation is currently a vigorously debated concept on all levels of librarianship and in all types of libraries, with the major research centers the prime targets. The question of academic status has become a rallying cry on the campus, almost on a level with other, infinitely more disruptive, but no less vital issues. And speaking of vital issues, what more surely represents our volatile world than the issue of intellectual freedom? Compared with these, the relatively stable concerns of professional education and of evaluating progress in libraries are indeed amenable, even though not uncomplicated. These, then, are the subjects we have chosen to bring together in one place and in one time. It is our thought that this collection of papers can give true perspective to the past, the present, and possibly the future of research libraries.

A word should also be said for the select group of Downs' own staff who conceived the idea of producing the book, who helped to plan it, and who served in many ways to bring it to completion. Dr. Lucien White, Associate University Librarian at the University of Illinois, deserves special commendation. Other members of his staff have essays elsewhere in the text, and their personal contributions will be readily identified. For the patience of my own staff, without which my part in the production of this book would have been impossible, I am extremely grateful.

My own awareness of Robert Downs goes back to 1946, when I first moved back to the central middle west. Very soon after taking up my work at Washington University in St. Louis, the proximity of the great library, a great librarian, and the library school at Urbana began to affect our professional development there. Staff interaction, professional counsel, material resources, all good things came to us through liberal cooperation in services and personal relationships encouraged by Downs. Later, during my years at the Air University in Alabama when I was reorganizing library service for the major educational enterprises of the U.S. Air Force, it was again his wise counsel as a member of my Advisory Board which steadied my impulsiveness. It was in my final and enduring move to the University of North Carolina that I found my greatest satisfaction in following in the footsteps of my venerated mentor, Louis R. Wilson, and my valued friend, Bob Downs. One could hardly ask for a greater challenge. If, as time goes on, my own work at North Carolina and elsewhere is noted with the achievements of these two great librarians, I will know that the challenge has been met.   J. O.

BIOGRAPHY OF ROBERT B. DOWNS

by Robert F. Delzell

Bob Downs was born on a farm in the Blue Ridge mountains of North Carolina, near Lenoir, with a combination of English, Scotch, and Dutch ancestry. His family had lived in North Carolina for many generations. His father, John McLeod Downs, did almost anything to avoid farming; at different times he ran a country store and a tannery. He became a state legislator, county commissioner, justice of the peace, and taught in the public schools and in schools of music in the area.

Bob lived on the farm until he was fourteen. For seven of those years he attended a one-room school. From the beginning he was surrounded by books; his father collected them, and the one-room school had a small library. Early exposure to the world's literature had its effect; Bob became and has continued to be an omnivorous reader. Difficult as it is to believe now, he was a high school dropout after one year. Tall in stature, with a rangy build, Bob worked for several years on a building construction project. For a time he was a fire ranger on Mt. Mitchell and then a telephone repairman for Southern Bell. He also worked as a ranch hand in Wyoming where his oldest brother lived.

In 1917 the Downs family moved to Asheville and Bob went with them. There he found the Asheville Public Library and for several years read his way through an average of a book a day. After drifting for a time, he went back to finish high school, taking his last year at Trinity High School, then on the site where Duke University now stands.

With high school out of the way, Bob went directly to the University of North Carolina at Chapel Hill. The year was 1923; he was a freshman and a student assistant in the university library. He hasn't been out of a library since. He has said many times that he was especially influenced by Louis Round Wilson, who later became University Librarian at Chapel Hill. After receiving his B.A. degree in Chapel Hill in 1926, Bob went on to the Columbia University Library School to obtain his B.S. and M.S. degrees in Library Science. While attending library school, he worked as a student assistant in the Columbia University Library and as a reference assistant in the New York Public Library.

In 1929 he married a classmate, the charming Elizabeth Crooks, who has devoted the years since to being wife, mother, colleague, and co-author. Their two daughters, Clara and Roberta, are married and have families of their own.

In 1929 he was named Librarian and Assistant Professor of Bibliography at Colby College, Waterville, Maine. Two years later he was invited to return to the University of North Carolina as Assistant Librarian and Associate Professor of Library Science. Louis Round Wilson left Chapel Hill in 1932 and Downs became Acting Librarian. In 1933 he was appointed University Librarian and Professor of Library Science. During his productive years in Chapel Hill, Bob developed strong collections in a number of areas and instituted an important program of duplicate exchanges. Then, as now, he was deeply concerned with service to undergraduate students. Along with his administrative duties, he found time to teach courses in areas of special interest: bibliography, history of books and libraries, and reference. He worked closely with the Library School at Chapel Hill, developing his innate sense of organization and direction, which he later applied when he became the head of the Library and the Library School at the University of Illinois. He was prominent in the creation of the cooperative relationship which still exists between Duke University and the University of North Carolina. Librarians, faculty, and students valued his concern for their problems and his quick understanding of the scholarly requirements of the university community.

He remained at North Carolina until 1938 when he was appointed Director of Libraries at New York University. This was a new and challenging position which had been created a few years earlier to provide central direction for seven loosely organized libraries. He created machinery for the centralization of technical department activities, records, and a union catalog. He guided the staff through a complete reorganization of the Washington Square Library, instituting many changes resulting in obvious improvements in service.

It was September of 1943 when Bob Downs arrived in Urbana to take over as Director of the University of Illinois Library and Library

School and to embark on a unique and long period of professional service and intellectual growth. His accomplishments at Urbana and in the profession, since 1943, are legendary and well documented. The University of Illinois Library, with over four million volumes on the Urbana campus, is known all over the world. The Library School (now called the Graduate School of Library Science) ranks with the best.

This is the Bob Downs that so many of us know today, Dean of Library Administration at the University of Illinois. He might more appropriately be named Dean of Academic Librarianship to the world-at-large. His influence extends far beyond the library profession and it is evident that he will continue to range far and wide, writing, lecturing, traveling, consulting, and living each day with commitment and an intellectual intensity far beyond ours. Retirement for Bob Downs should bring relief from schedules and the confining tensions of administration, with all the time he needs to do only what he wants to do.

Any review of the drives and interests which led Bob Downs to the notable accomplishments of his career, would have to begin with an early love of and desire to travel. He first went to Europe in 1925, between his junior and senior years in college. Since that time he has traveled to all of the continents with the single exception of Australia. It would not be unusual to find that he has eliminated this exception before this volume comes off the press.

In 1948 he was called to Japan to assist in the organization of the National Diet Library. He was acting as a special consultant to the Civil Information and Education Section of the General Headquarters of the Supreme Commander for the Allied Powers in Tokyo. Two years later, in 1950, he returned to Japan to organize the Japan Library School at Keio University. This project was financed by the Department of the Army, under the supervision and administration of the American Library Association.

The Rockefeller Foundation sent him to Mexico City in 1952 to act as consultant to the National Library and the University of Mexico in an examination of their organizational problems. His next jaunt abroad took him to Turkey where he directed the establishment of the Library School at Ankara. The Ford Foundation subsidized this operation for a number of years. He was called back to Turkey in 1968 by the Agency for International Development to advise on the spending of two large grants for the development of book collections at the Middle East Technical University and Hacettepe University in Ankara.

South America benefited from Bob Downs' professional presence on three different occasions. In 1960 he made a complete circuit of the continent in behalf of the Farmington Plan, making dealer contacts for future orders for Latin American publications. The State Department sent him to Brazil in 1962 to lecture at libraries and library schools in São Paulo, Rio de Janeiro, and Belo Horizonte. A Rockefeller Foundation Project took him to Medellín, Colombia, in 1964, where he acted as consultant to the Interamerican Library School.

A new trail was broken in 1963 when the Agency for International Development sent him to Afghanistan to plan a new library for the University of Kabul. In 1964–1965 he was consultant to the university library and new library school at the University of Puerto Rico. In 1968 he returned to Puerto Rico to give a series of lectures at the library school.

In the process of this considerable amount of international travel, the effective work of Bob Downs is evident in the appearance in other countries of improved library practices obviously based on practices developed in our own country. At the same time, his own professional and intellectual acumen grew and matured. The usefulness of work in the international community at any level cannot be denied and international personalities from library, educational, and government fields beat a constant path to the door of his office in the University of Illinois Library.

Resources of American libraries would have to be placed high on the list of Downs' professional concerns. He began working in this area as early as 1930. His contributions to the literature in this area are well documented in over ninety of his publications. *Resources of Southern Libraries* (1938), *Resources of New York City Libraries* (1942), *American Library Resources* (1951), *Resources of North Carolina Libraries* (1964), *Resources of Missouri Libraries* (1966), and *Resources of Canadian Academic and Research Libraries* (1967) are prominent examples of the careful, comprehensive surveys of research materials for which the scholarly world has often turned to Bob Downs with appreciation. During the period when he was teaching at the University of Illinois Library School, his course on resources of American libraries was eagerly sought by those students fortunate enough to be in school at that time. With content enough for two courses and his logical, comprehensive coverage of this huge mass of material, he gave students an insight into the organized mind that enabled him to plan and develop the methods with which the evaluation of scholarly library resources can be completed on a high level of competence. Perfection in any sort of survey work is always in question; there is always someone to argue that something has been left out or overemphasized. In this field, however, what has been done is done extremely well and, in all likelihood, better than if anyone else in the field had attempted it.

As an adjunct to the area of resources, Bob Downs has worked long and hard in the often arid fields of interlibrary cooperation. He was active in the founding and development of the Midwest Interlibrary Center (now called the Center for Research Libraries). While he vigorously supported the original concept of the Center, he has been openly critical of policies adopted by the Center, when he did not believe that they were in the best interests of all concerned.

The status of librarians has interested him since 1940. It was under his guidance in 1944 that a reorganization of the professional library staff at the University of Illinois was accomplished, and librarians were removed from the University Civil Service System and given full faculty rank and status. As the trend toward academic recognition of professional librarians grew, Bob examined the movement, commented on it, surveyed it, and continued to express his personal belief that librarians in academic institutions must be so recognized. Over the years librarians across the country have turned to Bob Downs for aid, comfort, and advice as they entered on the tortuous path to academic recognition in their own institutions. Downs believes that librarians should and can continue to prove that this recognition is warranted.

The cause of intellectual freedom has always been important to Downs. He was an eloquent spokesman when, as President of the American Library Association in 1952, it was necessary to respond to the infamous McCarthy campaign. Downs created the atmosphere, timing, and impetus for President Eisenhower's "don't burn the books" statement, which helped immeasurably to stem the tide of reactionary censorship. The American Library Association's freedom to read statement is perhaps even more important today than when it was drafted in 1952. *The First Freedom; Liberty and Justice in the World of Books and Reading*, published by the American Library Association in 1960, is Bob's compilation of the important writings on literary censorship. Many a librarian has reached for this volume when the censors took to their guns to shoot a book off the shelves of a library. One of his latest publications* constitutes a flawless statement on censorship. In it he reiterates his firm conviction that we must "remain a free people in the field of reading."

Over twenty institutions and organizations have called upon the

---

* Freedom of Speech and Press: Development of a Concept. In *Library Trends*, 19:1, pp. 8–18, July, 1970.

Downs expertise in the area of library surveys. Having accomplished so much in his state and country-wide examination of libraries, he has produced a continuing list of published and unpublished surveys of such individual libraries as Cornell University, the University of Utah, Purdue University, the Library Company of Philadelphia, Southern Illinois University, the University of Puerto Rico, Fisk University, the University of Cincinnati, and the Georgia Institute of Technology. He is currently working on a program survey for the new Governor's State University just south of Chicago, Illinois.

Throughout his active career, Bob Downs has worked at the endless task of building collections. This responsibility, which he accepts so readily and handles so well, is evident in each of the libraries where he was the responsible head. For the past twenty-seven years he has applied this talent to the University of Illinois Library. The results of his dedication to this aspect of librarianship are best recorded in his own comments on the collections at the University of Illinois Library.*

Downs has said that "a library is never finished. Research interests in a university are constantly changing."† Alert to these changes, he has guided Illinois into major new growth in foreign area studies. Following on the heels of the Farmington Plan, Illinois has been building actively in the Slavic language materials; since 1962 Illinois has participated in the Public Law 480 Program for Indian and Pakistani publications, and, starting in 1964, for Indonesian and United Arab Republic publications. The buildup of Chinese and Japanese materials by direct purchase is under way. During the past year, African and Afro-American Bibliographers were added to the Acquisition Department staff to develop collections in those areas.

In the growth and development of all collections in Urbana, Downs has worked closely with his Acquisition, Serials, and Special Languages staffs, with faculty specialists and specialist bibliographers. He understands fully the need for the closest kind of cooperative effort if coverage in any area is to be adequate for current and future needs.

American folklore, especially humor, has interested Bob Downs for the major part of his life. Folklore is indigenous to the area in which he spent his childhood and he must have heard hundreds of stories from the southern mountains as he grew up in North Carolina. With the collabora-

* The University of Illinois Library. In *Library Trends*, 15:2, pp. 258–265, October, 1966.
† *Ibid*, p. 263.

tion of his wife, Betty, he wrote a pamphlet on *American Humor* as early as 1937. He continued to write in this field and climaxed his efforts in 1964 with the publication of *The Bear Went Over the Mountain; Tall Tales of American Animals.* Those fortunate enough to have heard him read stories from this particularly delightful collection will attest to the dry wit and complete charm of his performance.

On the Urbana campus of the University of Illinois, Downs has been deeply involved in the curricular and extracurricular activities which are carried on in such abundance as to stagger many a campus administrator. He has found time to be Chairman of the Land Grant Centennial Committee; Vice-Chairman of the University of Illinois Centennial Committee; Chairman of the Senate Committee on Honorary Degrees, Chairman of the University Concert and Entertainment Board; President of the local chapters of Phi Beta Kappa and Phi Kappa Phi. He has been equally active in the community and has served as President of the Urbana Rotary Club.

On the campus and off, Bob Downs has had the honor of receiving many awards. Having served as President of the American Library Association, the Illinois Library Association, and the Association of College and Research Libraries, his name and reputation are well known far beyond the range of his profession.

He has received honorary degrees from Colby College, the University of North Carolina, the University of Toledo, and Ohio State University. In 1963 he won the American Library Association's Clarence Day Award and, in 1964, the Joseph W. Lippincott Award. I often think he was most pleased when he received the Brown Derby Award from the University of Illinois chapter of Sigma Delta Chi. This award, which Downs accepted in 1960, is given annually "to the faculty member who has made the greatest contribution to the University community in the past or recent years."

Some of Downs' most intense writing stems from his study of the influence of books. Beginning with a small pamphlet published in 1935, *The Story of Books,* he continued to write on this subject until he completed a book manuscript, published in 1956 with the title, *Books That Changed the World.* This title has been extremely well received; it has been published in at least ten different languages, including Vietnamese. In 1961 he published an enlarged version of this work under the title, *Molders of the Modern Mind.* His latest effort, *Books That Changed America,* is scheduled for publication in 1971. No doubt he will continue to write on this subject. Downs himself has said that he is a "compulsive scribbler"; compulsive perhaps, but not a scribbler. He writes with ease; his style is terse, clean, and readable. He synthesizes with skill, interprets with accuracy, and manages to bring to vivid life not only the book he is scrutinizing, but the author and the material as set against the time and country in which the book first appeared. Not many writers in this field are blessed with this talent for perception. Bob Downs has published over three hundred items and, currently, has ten in process.

I have known Bob Downs as an employer, colleague, mentor, and friend. We have worked together for over fifteen years with mutual respect, admiration, and confidence. He is quiet, thoughtful, and scholarly by nature. For these qualities to be mistaken for reserve is unfortunate. There is warmth, kindness, and humor behind the deep-set eyes. He can tell a shaggy dog story with consummate skill. I am grateful for my association with Bob.

The Clarence Day Award, for promoting the love of books and reading, given to Downs in 1963, bears a reliable brief description of the man:

> Robert Bingham Downs, Dean of Library Administration of the University of Illinois, is a distinguished administrator, author, lecturer, and teacher who has served librarianship with distinction at home and abroad. Throughout his career he has by example as well as in his teaching, speaking, and writing emphasized the love of books and reading. He has been a prolific writer; and whether he was at a given moment directing the libraries of Colby College, the University of North Carolina, New York University, or the University of Illinois, or in one of the furthermost corners of the earth, very probably he was also writing.
>
> Resources of American libraries, cooperation among research libraries, censorship, union catalogs, and international exchanges have received his attention with profit to all librarians and scholars. But in such works as *Books That Changed the World* (1956) and *Molders of the Modern Mind* (1961) he has reached out beyond the library profession and has led thousands of readers to the timeless books, the great classics of our civilization. For many it has been a second try, but for all it has been with deeper understanding and purpose. No other librarian has reached such a wide audience, and no other librarian has made a richer contribution to an understanding of books both for their enjoyment and for their significance for our time.

Current and future generations of librarians will find that they all owe something to Bob Downs. His life and professional contributions are woven so intricately into the fabric of librarianship that no one will remain untouched.

About the Author

Robert F. Delzell, long-time administrative assistant to Bob Downs and now Director of Personnel for the University of Illinois Library, is eminently qualified by this experience to write the biographical sketch. A brilliant undergraduate, Delzell began in publishing work, moved early into the library field and rapidly to administration. His formal library training at Illinois brought him to Downs' attention, and after a brief series of working experiences in other large libraries, Downs brought him back to Illinois in administrative support. Legman and dedicated lieutenant for Downs for more than a dozen years, Delzell's affection and esteem for him are apparent in his essay.

RESEARCH
LIBRARIANSHIP

INTELLECTUAL FREEDOM

by Everett T. Moore

On May 22, 1953, the *New York Times* reported that the flow of American books to the State Department's libraries abroad had "slowed to a trickle" while department officials tried to work out a system for barring works by Communist authors. The problem, officials said, was one of setting up a workable procedure for evaluating information which was being turned up on authors under investigation to determine whether their works came within the limitations laid down by direction of Secretary of State John Foster Dulles. Up to that time, a "relatively small number" of contemporary writers, estimated at around a hundred, had been cleared.

Lawrence Wadsworth, former Chief Deputy of Public Affairs in the State Department's Far Eastern Bureau, had said the day before in a speech in Washington that at the time of his resignation, three weeks earlier, the department's library director was "still investigating to determine whether the works of Adlai E. Stevenson, Democratic Presidential candidate in 1952, would come within policy limitations."

This nightmarish report was one of many that had been appearing in the news for some weeks concerning the frantic efforts being made by State Department officials to satisfy the demands of Senator Joseph R. McCarthy's Senate Subcommittee on Investigations. They demanded that the overseas information libraries of the State Department be purged of "the works of all Communist authors, any publication continually publishing Communist propaganda, and questionable material lending undue emphasis to Communist personalities or their statements." Such

1

were the words of the department's "weeding out" directive issued on March 18, 1953.

Senator McCarthy's investigators, Roy M. Cohn and G. David Schine, had been touring the U.S. Information Service libraries in Europe and reported finding many books on the libraries' shelves that presented "pro-Communist" viewpoints or were written by authors "known" to be Communists. Since these libraries were key elements in the U.S. government's overseas propaganda services directed by the USIS (then a branch of the State Department), Senator McCarthy considered this evidence as confirming his accusations that the department was mined with Communists and Communist sympathizers and that the best interests of the nation were being dangerously—even treasonably—subverted.

The attack on the libraries was, therefore, centered on the question of what authors were being stocked in the 194 information libraries in sixty-one countries and how these authors' works had been selected. In April of that year, Senator McCarthy had "urged" Secretary Dulles to trace those responsible for placing such controversial books in overseas libraries, asking in a letter for a report on who accepted the books, if they were gifts, and whether such persons were still in the State Department. He complained of noncooperation from some of former Secretary Dean Acheson's "lieutenants" in the department, remarking that the "old Acheson team" displayed bad memories. One State Department man denied that any pro-Communist books had been "planted" in libraries. He said a few books on the disapproved list had been donated, but none were bought. Senator McCarthy felt particularly frustrated on this point, saying in a televised hearing that his subcommittee had been unable to fix responsibility for the acquisition of controversial books for the information libraries. The source of the Senator's frustration seemed to be his assumption that some kind of subversive plot was at work which included in its schemes a policy on selecting books that would slyly bring to the shelves of the overseas libraries those very books that would degrade the United States before the world and glorify Communism. In the nation's own citadels of propaganda, the Communist message would be given top billing.

Viewing the noisy and brutal interlude in retrospect, it is apparent that McCarthy's investigators did a woefully unprofessional job of assessing the causes for the presence on USIS library shelves of books that offended them. The "I-have-here-a-list" technique that the Senator adopted as one of his trademarks in subsequent hearings was employed here just as it was in identifying "subversives" in the employ of the government. It was the *authors* of the books, not their ideas, that were the visible targets. On the basis, therefore, that Dashiell Hammett had been jailed for six months in 1951 for contempt of court, *The Thin Man* and all his other books were unacceptable for overseas libraries. Similarly unacceptable were Howard Fast's historical novels, because the author was "identified with left-wing activities" and·in 1950 had been jailed for contempt of Congress. Also, all the work of William Gropper, artist and muralist, who on May 6, 1953 had invoked the Fifth Amendment before Senator McCarthy's subcommittee. The books of Lawrence K. Rosinger, specialist on Far Eastern affairs, who in 1952 had declined to tell Senate investigators if he had ever been a Communist, were also condemned. Similar treatment was accorded the books of such writers as Herbert Aptheker, Millen Bran, Earl Browder, Helen Goldfrank, Morris V. Schappes, Bernard J. Stern, and Gene Weltfish—some of them Communists, others with records of being "uncooperative" before Congressional investigators.

One blacklisted writer, Edgar Snow, author of *Red Star Over China,* wrote to the *New York Times* (June 16, 1953): "In these times it is no joke to appear on any 'blacklist,' much less to have one's name published on a State Department list of demerited political delinquents—with inferences of a subversive character which can be seriously damaging to one's professional as well as personal interests.

"I have been a newspaper man, war correspondent, and author," Snow wrote, "who has worked abroad more or less continuously since 1928, shortly after I left the Missouri School of Journalism. My reports are in themselves an open record that I have at no time been a politician or an adherent of any political party but have been solely concerned with ascertaining and interpreting the facts in any given situation to the best of my ability and have been satisfied to let historians—in which category I do not include intellectual stowaways such as Cohn, Schine, and McCarthy—assess their accuracy and value. . . ."

Snow noted that all of his books were banned in the Soviet Union and the satellite countries, and those published before 1942 had been banned in Germany and Japan.

There were, in all, more than forty authors whose several hundred books had been removed from the shelves of the overseas libraries. The *New York Times* found, through a survey conducted by its correspondents in twenty capitals of the world, that the State Department had issued at least six confidential directives to the libraries between February 19 and June 21, in 1953, concerning the purge. No single specific instruction covered all the withdrawals. The *Times* reported that "The nearest to a common factor appeared to be refusal to tell Federal investigators about Communist affiliation." Also cited were instances of authors' criticism of U.S. policy in the Far East.

Walter Sullivan, reporting to the *Times* from Berlin, on June 11, 1953, wrote of the effect of the book banning on the forty USIS libraries in Berlin and West Germany, the prestigious "Amerika Hauser," which were showplaces of American library service. "These and other recent developments in Germany have done much to undo the herculean efforts of the United States occupation forces in the post-war years to present American democracy to the German people as a magnet to draw them away from totalitarian attitudes," he wrote. One such development, he said, was the report that State Department investigators were questioning all who attended the recent farewell party in Bonn for Theodore Kaghan, former chief of the information division in the High Commissioner's office. Kaghan had been forced to resign after being recalled to testify before Senator McCarthy's subcommittee. Reports from Bonn told of pressure put on some of those known to have attended the party to furnish lists of names of others seen there.

In assessing the impact of this set of events we need to consider the position of the overseas libraries in the larger scheme of American library service. Were these typical American public libraries? They were not intended to be, for they were designed to serve the U.S. Government in its efforts to provide people in other countries with information about the United States—our people, our institutions, our commerce and industry, our cultural life. They were an outgrowth of the libraries established during World War II under the Office of War Information in principal cities of Allied countries. After the war, the State Department assumed responsibility for the program, and by the 1950s, libraries had been established in many countries of the world. Additionally, military governments in Germany and Japan opened libraries in those countries during the occupation periods, after which the State Department took these over also.

The successful pattern of the wartime libraries was carried over to the new system of libraries, with well-qualified professional librarians directing them. The libraries did employ such features of our public libraries as could appropriately be applied in overseas situations: open shelves, card catalogs, reference assistance, comfortable and inviting reading rooms, and, most important, books and periodicals selected with a view to representing a variety of viewpoints and with no arbitrary restrictions imposed as to ideological views of authors.

The philosophy had been one of letting American books speak for themselves without fearing the possibility of conveying unconventional or even dangerous thoughts from author to reader. This in itself was considered an important demonstration of American faith in free dissemination of thought.

The overseas libraries have, therefore, been considered by some observers of our efforts abroad to be the most legitimate of all our propaganda programs. If our present overseas programs (now conducted by the U.S. Information Agency, an independent office which replaced the USIS in 1953) produce a lot of noise and perhaps win few hearts and minds with their propaganda, as one critic has recently charged, we may still look to the USIA libraries as conveying a kind of quiet but powerful message through their presence as useful and trustworthy organs of information. For, although their book selection policies may still reflect some of the timidity engendered by the Cohn–Schine investigations, and although USIA Director Frank Shakespeare's instruction to the libraries, sent out early in 1970, to order certain "conservative" books if their existing collections were "preponderantly liberal" betrays a sad misapprehension as to the art of developing a balanced and representative collection of books, the overseas libraries do a remarkably good job of representing our principles of free access to ideas.

The combined McCarthy–State Department attack on the principle of selecting books according to their individual values rather than by the personal beliefs of their authors was therefore a direct attack on American library purposes and practices. The overseas libraries were highly regarded by the American library profession, and although it was acknowledged that there was an essential distinction, as William Dix pointed out in an address to the New York Library Association in October, 1953, "between the completely free operation of libraries in this country and the Government's choice of books for its overseas libraries, since the latter was a matter of strategy and tactics in the cold war," the threat to our principles of free selection and free access to ideas was recognized as striking at home as well as abroad. The challenge to American librarianship was accepted, and the events of the latter weeks of June and the first weeks of July of 1953 are among the most notable in our history.

The American Library Association was already on record as opposed to "labeling" of books in libraries. On July 13, 1951, its Council had unanimously adopted the "Statement on Labeling," in which the librarians declared that the technique of labeling is an attempt to prejudice the reader, and that the presence of a book or magazine in a library does not indicate an endorsement of its contents by the library. "Libraries do not advocate the ideas found in their collections," the statement said. The action had been prompted by efforts that had been made in a number of communities to force librarians to remove from their shelves, or to label, books and magazines considered controversial or subversive, and to boycott booksellers and publishers dealing in such materials. Among the proposals was one to label "all subversive material" in the Library of Congress. Another was to remove publications of the United Nations and UNESCO from school libraries, and the branding in red ink "in letters an inch high" of all Communist or "subversive" material kept in research libraries.

In San Antonio, Texas, in May 1953, the organizer of the San Antonio Minute Women presented to the City Council a list of 600 books, allegedly by Communist sympathizers, with the recommendation that the books "be stamped on the inside cover with a red stamp, large enough to be seen immediately, showing that the author has Communist front affiliations, and the number of citations." Included on the list were Einstein's *Theory of Relativity*, Thomas Mann's *Magic Mountain* and *Joseph in Egypt*, Norbert Wiener's *Cybernetics*, and a variety of books on the arts, anthologies of folk songs, books on the mentally ill, child care, and alcoholics, and mystery novels. The librarian barely survived the controversy engendered in the community by these proposals, but the list was used by Minute Women and other volunteer censor groups across the country to press for banning or labeling of books in public and school libraries. The most famous advocate of "voluntary book-burning—the only kind we will ever have in the United States" was Mrs. Anne Smart, who, a year later, led a crusade in Marin County, California, to censor and label books in school libraries. The ALA's Statement on Labeling was not accepted as doctrine in many communities.

The Chairman of the ALA's Intellectual Freedom Committee in 1953, William S. Dix, reported that more than a hundred communities in the country were experiencing some kind of pressures by would-be censors to apply restrictions to libraries' freedom of selection and freedom of access. The attacks on the American libraries abroad were an extension of a movement which had already gained strong momentum at home. Senator Joseph McCarthy himself was aware of the controversy over the placing of pro-Soviet material in public libraries. Had not the Boston *Post,* in September of 1952, called attention to the fact that the Senator's own book *McCarthyism and the Fight for America; Documented Answers to Questions Asked by Friend and Foe* (1952) was not available in the Boston Public Library when the *Post* started serializing it? The paper went on to charge (accurately) in subsequent issues that the library had files of the *New World Review, Pravda,* and *Izvestia—* not on open shelves, but available on request—and had even included in a lobby display arranged by the Great Books Foundation a copy of Karl Marx's *Communist Manifesto.* The resultant controversy over purchase of Communist materials brought the library's Board of Trustees close to adopting a policy prohibiting it, but this move was finally defeated.

Now, in 1953, when Senator McCarthy was asserting that American libraries overseas were being used by the State Department to betray the American cause in the world, librarians and book publishers saw this as a threat to the freedom to read—not only for peoples of other countries in which the information libraries were maintained, but for the American people at home. In May of that year, therefore, some thirty leaders of the American Library Association and the American Book Publishers Council held a meeting to consider what action they might take to counter the threat posed by the Senator, who appeared to be receiving effective, if frightened, cooperation from State Department

officials. The product of the meeting was the now famous statement on "The Freedom to Read"—famous because it is perhaps the most eloquent statement of principle we have had on this subject in our time, and because it has in the years since then been a powerful document in the fight against censorship. (The ALA's Intellectual Freedom Committee had also held a meeting—a special institute convened just before the annual ALA Conference—to consider the problems of applying the association's principles and to work at resolving differences of opinion among librarians, for there was far from uniform agreement on the application of the accepted general principles.)

"The Freedom to Read" statement asserted that "Private groups and public authorities in various parts of the country are working to remove books from sale, to censor textbooks, to label 'controversial' books, to distribute lists of 'objectionable' books or authors, and to purge libraries. These actions apparently rise from a view that our national tradition of free expression is no longer valid; that censorship and suppression are needed to avoid the subversion of politics and the corruption of morals. We, as citizens devoted to the use of books and as librarians and publishers responsible for disseminating them, wish to assert the public interest in the freedom to read."

A matter of much note, coming shortly after the ALA–ABPC conference, was President Dwight D. Eisenhower's denunciation of "book burners" and thought control in his informal response at the Dartmouth College commencement and baccalaureate service on June 14, when an honorary degree was conferred on him. The *New York Times* wrote that the President's words took on particular significance "because he talked in a venerable seat of learning."

"Don't join the book burners," the President said. "Don't think you are going to conceal faults by concealing evidence that they ever existed. Don't be afraid to go in your library and read every book as long as any document does not offend our own ideas of decency. That should be the only censorship.

"How will we defeat Communism unless we know what it is? What it teaches—why does it have such an appeal for men? Why are so many people swearing allegiance to it? It's almost a religion, albeit one of the nether regions."

The *Times* observed editorially that "If it is a suspicious sign for an American citizen to wish to know something about Communism, then the 33,938,285 citizens who voted for Dwight D. Eisenhower last November are guilty by association."

In Congress, the *Times* reported a few days later, "the reaction was mixed, and Senator Joseph R. McCarthy, Wisconsin Republican, said he did not believe that the President's speech was directed at him. The State Department announced that no order had been issued to burn or destroy books assailed by Senator McCarthy. 'Anyone who did anything about destroying a book,' said a department spokesman, 'did so under his own initiative. . . .' As for the genesis of the speech itself, a canvass of persons closely associated with the President for months indicated that it was pure unadulterated Eisenhower. No ghost writers, no advisers prepared a text or notes, or coined phrases for the President. All the evidence obtained today indicated that . . . [it] welled up as the expression of a deep-felt philosophy, and was stirred by recent inquiries into books and persons."

The next day, the *Times* reported that President Eisenhower "turned aside efforts to point his Sunday speech at Senator Joseph McCarthy, saying he never dealt in personalities." He said he favored the destruction of books advocating the overthrow of the U.S. Government that might be in libraries overseas. He viewed their retention as silly, placing the Government in the position of being a party to self-destruction. He defended the retention of "merely controversial books" in any American library, whether overseas or at home.

Senator McCarthy had said that President Eisenhower could not very well have been referring to him. "I have burned no books. It's impossible to know to whom he was referring." He said that Administration officials had ordered the removal of books by Communist authors from State Department libraries, adding that "obviously he agrees with what his Cabinet officers are doing or he would countermand their orders."

It was at about that time that Secretary of State Dulles had disclosed that in response to the department's order to remove books by Communist authors or sympathizers a few books actually had been burned, but that orders had subsequently gone out to burn no more.

An official of the department said the book purge in the overseas libraries had been "exaggerated out of all proportions." But other officials in Washington expressed shock that the Government was burning books at all, literally or figuratively. There were denials that any "black-list" had been issued. It was difficult to approach the purge issue on the basis of a broad, all-encompassing directive, one official said. The staff man out in Bangkok, it was suggested, was on the spot if he was expected to know which authors were Communists or fellow travelers, though directives from Washington had said they, as authors, should be eliminated. Meanwhile, Senator McCarthy's subcommittee was preparing its detailed report on Communist authors whose books had been spotted on the shelves of the information libraries. This would be the closest to an "all-encompassing" blacklist that would appear.

This was the state of affairs when the American Library Association gathered in Los Angeles toward the end of June, 1953, for its conference. The *New York Times* said in an editorial that "No more appropriate time could be chosen for the convening of a large group of librarians than during this period when books and book selection policies of American libraries at home and abroad have been brought into question by various congressional committees and freelance censors. For years the American Library Association and its members have been fighting to perpetuate the idea of true intellectual freedom and have developed the 'Library Bill of Rights,' which freed librarians from strictures in their book selection and more or less guaranteed the rights of libraries to present both sides of the question on all controversial issues. . . . Now . . . librarians once more will be called upon to affirm their faith in the presentation of all sides of issues in library collections."

The *Times* hoped that people in the United States would follow the lead of the librarians and take courage "to continue the battle against 'book burners' and self-appointed censors who have so little faith in the American people that they would eliminate their free right to choose."

At the opening session of the ALA conference, Robert B. Downs, the President, who was Director of Libraries and Dean of the Library School of the Univerversity of Illinois and a member of the State Department's Committee on Books Abroad, said, "A virulent disease, presently diagnosed as 'McCarthyism,' but antedating [by centuries] the distinguished Senator for whom it is named, is infecting nearly every segment of our Governmental structure, from national down to local levels."

"Look, for example," said Dr. Downs, "at the excellent system of

194 information libraries now operated by the Department of State in some sixty-one foreign countries. Stringent censorship directives, issued in the atmosphere of fear, hysteria, and repression now prevailing in Washington, threaten to place the entire information library program in jeopardy. . . . It seems that if any derogatory information, no matter how irresponsible, exists about a writer, his books cannot be used in the information program. Works in such presumably non-controversial fields as medicine and mathematics are not excepted. Among recent books to fall under suspicion and investigation are those by such prominent Americans as Adlai Stevenson, the Rev. A. Powell Davies, Judge Learned Hand, George Gershwin, and Secretary of State Dulles himself. It is not difficult to imagine the impression which the audience whom the information libraries are trying to reach is gaining of freedom of speech and of the press in the United States."

Copies of the "Freedom to Read" statement were distributed to the members of the ALA Council, and on June 25 that body unanimously voted its endorsement. The American Book Publishers Council's board of directors had given its endorsement to the statement the week before.

In reporting this action, the *New York Times* revealed that the document had been drafted by a committee appointed by the group who had met under ALA–ABPC auspices in Rye, New York, on May 2 and 3 (hence the name of "The Westchester Statement" informally given to it). The drafting committee was composed of Luther H. Evans, Librarian of Congress; Douglas M. Black, President of Doubleday & Co., and of the ABPC; William S. Dix, Librarian of Princeton University and Chairman of the ALA's Committee on Intellectual Freedom; Dr. Downs; Arthur A. Houghton, Jr., President of Steuben Glass, Inc.; Harold Lasswell, Professor of Law and Political Science at the Yale University Law School; John Cory, Chief of the New York Public Library's Circulation Department; and Dan Lacy, Managing Director of the ABPC.

Dr. Downs and Mr. Black said in a joint statement to the press, "The librarians and publishers of America demonstrate their support of President Eisenhower's warning at Dartmouth, 'Don't join the bookburners.' "

President Eisenhower himself wrote to Dr. Downs during the ALA conference commending "the precious liberties of our nation: freedom of inquiry, freedom of the spoken and the written word, freedom of exchange of ideas."

"We must in these times," the President wrote, "be intelligently alert not only to the fanatic cunning of Communist conspiracy—but also to the grave dangers in meeting fanaticism with ignorance. For, in order to fight totalitarians who exploit the ways of freedom to serve their own ends, there are some zealots who—with more wrath than wisdom— would adopt a strangely unintelligent course. They would try to defend freedom by denying freedom's friends the opportunity of studying Communism in its entirety—its plausibilities, its falsities, its weaknesses."

This time, when Senator McCarthy was asked whether he found in this letter any reference to himself, he declined to comment.

The ALA Council, at the conference in Los Angeles, also adopted a ringing "Overseas Library Statement," noting that the State Department's Information Administration "must be free to use in its libraries whatever books its responsible professional judgment determines are necessary or useful to the provision of such a service. To deny itself the tools it needs to serve the United States for irrelevant reasons of the past associations of authors and in fear of domestic criticism is indefensible."

"The American overseas libraries," said the Council, "do not belong to a Congressional Committee or to the State Department. They belong to the whole American people, who are entitled to have them express their finest ideals of responsible freedom. In no other way can the libraries effectively serve their purpose, and in no other pattern can this Association aid their progress."

At week's end, on the day after the ALA's delegates dispersed, trailing firm statements on censorship and much eloquent defense of the freedom to read, Senator McCarthy's investigators announced that Rockwell Kent, the painter, Lillian Hellman, the playwright, and Dorothy Parker, the writer, were among twenty-three persons to be called as possible witnesses the following week to testify on the State Department's overseas libraries and information centers. Roy M. Cohn, chief counsel for the Senate Subcommittee on Investigations, said that he was having great difficulty locating some of the witnesses. It was obvious they were "ducking" his subpoenas, he said. Others called for the hearing were Mrs. Paul Robeson, wife of the singer, Richard O. Boyer, writer, Corliss Lamont, teacher and writer, and former New York University Professor Edwin B. Burgum.

Senator McCarthy said the additional authors were being called to "give a more complete picture" of the library program and to show the views of some of the writers whose books had been used. He said the hearings might also clear up some of the "confusion" over the book-burning charges.

By this time it was not surprising to see such names as these appear on the Senator's list of suspects. Rockwell Kent, prolific illustrator of books, and himself a writer, was known to have liberal, perhaps 'leftist' leanings, but he denied being a Communist or fellow traveler. Lillian Hellman described herself as a militant anti-Fascist. She was a movie scenarist as well as playwright, whose best known plays were "The Children's Hour," "Watch on the Rhine," and "The Little Foxes." Dorothy Parker, best known for her verse and short stories, had recently been writing screen scenarios in Hollywood. She had achieved special distinction there by being listed by the California State Senate's Un-American Activities Committee among a number of film writers, actors, and directors as having appeased Communism or followed the party line. Mrs. Paul Robeson, a writer and lecturer on race relations, published *African Journey* in 1945. Corliss Lamont, author of *The Peoples of the Soviet Union* (1946), had been chairman of the National Council of American–Soviet Friendship, but he denied being a Communist, saying that he was a "free wheeling American radical." Senator McCarthy's concept of "Communist" or "pro-Communist" writers would readily embrace authors such as these.

Occasional intrusions of comedy, though of somewhat grim quality, lightened the scene. When it was discovered that Whittaker Chambers' book *Witness,* an account of the Alger Hiss case from the standpoint of the man largely responsible for bringing the case about, had been removed from the Abraham Lincoln Library in Buenos Aires, Senator McCarthy threatened to raise the roof. He charged that someone in the State Department was trying to "sabotage" the purge program to make it look ridiculous. State Department officials explained that some errors might have been made, what with having to handle millions of books and periodicals. Librarians and their short staffs, they said, had been doing their best to follow orders to screen their shelves.

About a week later, Dr. Robert L. Johnson, chief of the State Department's International Information Administration, resigned. It was reported that he was quite ill, and that his condition had been aggravated by the strenuous nature of his assignment. When he had left the presidency of Temple University he had hoped to stay on in his new job indefinitely, but in his letter to President Eisenhower he said "the strains of his position were proving too much for him."

It was noted by the *New York Times* on July 7 that although his programs had been under constant scrutiny and attack, Dr. Johnson personally had fared well with the Congressional investigators. He had won the support of Senator McCarthy himself when the purge of books by Communists and fellow travelers had been called for, and also of Senator Bourke B. Hickenlooper, who had made a comprehensive investigation of the State Department's information activities. It was, rather, from the White House point of view, the *Times* said, that "the vast activities under Dr. Johnson, including the Voice of America, appeared to lack the drive and the lift that had been looked for when the Eisenhower Administration took office.

"The indecisive policy regarding the nature of the books that should be in the libraries, designed to explain the United States in foreign countries, was strongly disappointing at the White House," the *Times* said. "Two weeks ago Dr. Johnson said in a news conference that ten different directives had been issued in the effort to clarify the book issue and that the eleventh was being prepared." That eleventh directive, said the *Times,* apparently was spoiled by the President himself, who had remarked in a news conference that he would not have discarded mystery stories by Dashiell Hammett from the overseas libraries. "The fact that they had been removed," he added, "indicated that somebody in the library system had become frightened because Hammett was one of those who invoked constitutional privileges in refusing to say whether he had ever been a Communist."

Senator McCarthy praised Dr. Johnson for his "cooperation" with the Senate Permanent Subcommittee on Investigations. He hoped the Government would get as good a man to replace him. It was known by this time that the State Department's information activities probably would soon be transferred to an independent agency to be known as the U.S. Information Agency, as proposed by the President in a reorganization plan, but this was still subject to Congressional approval. A question then being asked in Washington was whether Senator McCarthy would continue investigating the information program after it came under the President's wing. The question could never be effectively answered, for Senator McCarthy was before long to meet his own doom at the hands of his fellow Senators.

Shortly after Dr. Johnson's resignation, however, the Eisenhower Administration sought to clarify its position on the Overseas Book and Library Program in a policy statement that called book burning a "wicked symbolic act" which was not to be condoned. The yardstick for selection was to be "the usefulness of a particular book in meeting the particularized needs of a particular area." The content was to be the important thing now, and such books conceivably might be the product of Communists if perchance they affirmatively served the ends of democracy, the statement said. Book selection policies would be based on the recommendations of carefully selected advisory committees composed of persons of unimpeachable reputation who were experts in their respective fields. Dr. Johnson, who submitted the statement, said it had the approval of Secretary Dulles.

Senator McCarthy's reaction was predictable. He said that to condone the Communist as author was "completely ridiculous"—that a Communist, under the discipline of the Party, would at all times advance the Communist cause, and that to accept any book by one of them would be "giving our stamp of approval" to it, and would contribute indirectly to the Communist Party. The Senator requested Dr. Johnson to appear before his subcommittee and asked that he bring with him "a list of those Communists whose writings you feel 'serve the ends of democracy' and an 'estimate' of the amount of 'taxpayers' money you would like to have appropriated to purchase and maintain the works of Communists which 'serve the ends of democracy.' " He also suggested that Dr. Johnson bring with him "the individual or individuals responsible for the decision to continue the purchase of books by Communist authors." (It had only recently been pointed out that books by Communist authors had not been bought by the information program, but had been "inherited" from the surplus of other Government libraries—presumably Army libraries overseas—and had not been sufficiently screened.)

Dr. Johnson attempted to clarify the policy statement on the Communist-as-author matter, saying, "This passage should be read in the context which makes it clear that we have no use for books which advocate, directly or indirectly, the undermining of our institutions." I quote from the statement: " 'These libraries are in business to advance American democracy, not Communist conspiracy.' "

It was late now for explanation, and it was apparent that no additional policy statements were going to help undo the damage that had been done, though this latest one did acknowledge the grievous errors committed by the people in the Information Service in attempting to satisfy Senator McCarthy's desire for purification of the State Department.

The death of McCarthyism could not yet be declared. Nor does it seem proper in the 1970s to say that it is yet dead. As Dr. Downs said, this "virulent disease, presently diagnosed as McCarthyism," antedated the Senator by centuries. He has recently referred to it, in the "Intellectual Freedom" issue of *Library Trends* (July 1970), as an even more virulent epidemic than that of the raids on Russian, Finnish, Polish, German, Italian, and other workmen, looking for Communists to deport, carried on under the direction of A. Mitchell Palmer, U.S. Attorney General, in 1920. And, he says, it is an epidemic "from which the nation has not yet fully recovered."

Out of the agonies of 1953, it should be remembered, came the librarians' clearest understanding of the threat of official repression when factors combine to give power to an unscrupulous politician. The statement on "The Freedom to Read" voiced that understanding in remarkable fashion. During the ALA conference at Los Angeles, the *New York Times* had said in an editorial that this statement and the resolution on overseas libraries "ought to be prominently displayed and readily available in every public library at home or abroad."

"The people of this country have too long endured the creeping threat of censorship over what they should be allowed to say or print or read or, by inference, think," the *Times* said. "Under the excuse of fighting authoritarian systems we have been urged to adopt one of the chief devices of authoritarianism, with the argument that if we do not accept these inquisitions we will fall into some kind of tyranny. Little men with narrow minds and with great lust for power have tried to dictate to us. To many of us, and obviously to those who drew up the Library Association's documents and those who voted to endorse them, these censors are in contempt of the most sacred traditions of American freedom. . . .

"The librarians at Los Angeles produced and accepted in their manifesto a document that seems today to belong, civilian and unofficial though it is, with America's outstanding state papers. It belongs there because of the nobility and courage of its expression, because it rests on experience, because it grew out of knowledge, not out of emotion, because it came from individuals who have found out day by day, in ill-paid and obscure positions, what the thinking people of this country really want. . . . ."

About the Author

Everett T. Moore is a distinguished example of Downs' ability to reach out to touch able men, wherever they may be. A native Californian, but not addicted, Moore leaped from Los Angeles to Harvard, to Berkeley, to Illinois, and finally settled in his home town, where he is now Assistant University Librarian at UCLA. He has been an outstanding leader for the cause of intellectual freedom, and has edited the ALA *Newsletter on Intellectual Freedom* and its monograph *Issues of Freedom in American Libraries*. He served Downs, Illinois, and the profession ably as issue editor of the July, 1970, *Library Trends* on "Intellectual Freedom." Everett Moore is unquestionably the paramount author to write on this subject today.

STATUS OF THE UNIVERSITY LIBRARIAN
IN THE ACADEMIC COMMUNITY

by Arthur M. McAnally

The emergence of academic librarianship as a profession has been a very long and sometimes tortuous process. The story begins about one hundred years ago when only two university libraries in the entire nation possessed as many as 50,000 volumes. Despite these small beginnings, early recognition of the importance of libraries in the educational process, and, consequently, the need for vigorous scholar-librarians qualified to be partners with the classroom faculty, appeared in the late 1800s in the writing of creative librarians such as Justin Winsor, professors such as the celebrated Henry James, and university presidents such as Daniel Coit Gilman at Johns Hopkins.[1] The first proposal that academic librarianship should be a profession in its own right may have been expressed by H. A. Sawtelle in 1878, when he stated that a good librarian must inspire and guide students in the use of library materials, a task which requires "no small amount of understanding and skill." He then concluded that the librarianship "ought not to be annexed to a professorship, but be itself a professorship."[2]

However, these admirable proposals of the 1870s to 1890s were more visionary than practical. Academic librarians were far from ready for such an educational role and would not be for many years. These early men of vision recognized a real need for qualified college and university librarians, and their suggestions were important to the development of an academic library profession. But a great many years were to elapse before the right kind of people were to be available.

OBSTACLES TO PROFESSIONALISM

Development of academic librarianship as a profession was impeded by many factors. Perhaps the first was the small size of library collections and, consequently, the small numbers of persons involved. As late as 1900, there were only a few hundred college and university librarians. A second factor was equally important—the low status of the profession itself. The principal concerns of librarians seemed to be housekeeping, or the mechanics of keeping the books—ordering, cataloging, and classifying them. There was little concern with utilization; the first "reference librarian" was not to be appointed until well after the turn of the century. There was little thought given to the contents of books or to the educational role of the library within the institution. The concept that library service was important to quality education was yet to emerge and be accepted.

Concerned as they were with housekeeping tasks, most of these early librarians rarely recognized any differences in level of duties to be performed. Everything that was done in a library was librarianship. Consequently, they did not separate clerical from professional tasks. Many library staffs consisted of ninety to one hundred percent "professionals" (if they could be found and hired), though perhaps three fourths of academic library tasks are routine and clerical in nature. This tended to inhibit the recruitment of persons with imagination, liveliness, and intellectual curiosity, thereby compounding the recruitment problem and impeding progress. It was not until 1927 that George Works first called national attention to the seriousness of this clerical–professional problem.[3]

This housekeeping approach, and the failure to distinguish between professional and clerical tasks, had two serious consequences. One effect was to hold down salaries, a very damaging situation. The other was the predominance of women in libraries. Library tasks seemed to be well suited to women, who also would work for small salaries. However, this was in an era when women were not really accepted as equal colleagues in the home, much less at work. The effect on attitudes of the academic community and especially the faculty, which certainly did not then recognize equality of the sexes and hardly does even today, was far-reaching.

Another handicap, and a very serious one, was the low quality of training for librarianship itself. The first library school did not come into existence until 1887. When it began, the principal concern was mechanics, with little attention to the social or educational role of the library. Housekeeping seemed to be what was wanted and needed most, and training in that was what librarians got.[4] It is astonishing how long this housekeeping attitude persisted—almost until our time. There also was far too much general training in these early schools, as they tended to train for the lowest common denominator of need. Furthermore, only a certificate was given or perhaps a bachelor's degree; there was no doctoral program in library science anywhere until 1928 when the Graduate Library School was established at the University of Chicago. Considerable cleaning up of library education followed the well-known Williamson report of 1923.[5] But library education did not begin to equal that of other professions (with the exception of the Chicago school) until the reforms of the 1940s, seventy years after these promising early proposals.

Still another inhibiting factor, and a very powerful one, was the attitude of the faculty toward librarians. This certainly is not surprising in the light of the liabilities noted above. Since librarians had little concern with educational or intellectual affairs, since so much of their work was obviously at a low clerical and housekeeping level, the profession dominated by women, and library education so miserable, they just were not qualified to be colleagues. The driving power of the housekeeping factor is demonstrated, curiously, by a statement in a little H. W. Wilson Company publication that "in the old days," librarians used to be told firmly that "he who reads is lost!" That is, librarians had too much work to be done to have time to read.[6] Thus it was not necessary for librarians to read; in fact, reading was "a positive crime." Great improvements were going to have to be made in the level of academic librarianship before faculty attitudes would change. With such a poor start, the process was to require a long time. This unwillingness of the classroom faculty to accept librarians as colleagues was to prove a very strong deterrent to the development of the profession. This attitude still persists to some extent today.[7] The inhibiting role of faculty opinion as recently as 1966–

1967 is revealed in the study by Schiller, which shows that the more conservative institutions are the slowest of all to grant academic status to professional librarians.[8] Blackburn suggests that there also are fundamental bases for conflict or competition between librarians and the classroom faculty, without offering any good ways to reduce them.[9] How serious these conflicts may be is questionable.

The bureaucratic structure of university library administration also has been a handicap. Early university libraries, lacking a well-educated staff capable of participation in policy decisions about library affairs or the educational role of the library in the institution, tended to develop vigorous chief librarians of an autocratic type. More recently, the chief librarian was a benevolent autocrat, but in a democracy all dictatorships are dangerous. One-man leadership has its perils, and a bureaucracy always resists change.[10] Changes that must be made in library administration to bring it into conformity with academic administration generally, essential if the entire library staff is to function as a true faculty,[11] tend to be opposed by some chief librarians—sometimes consciously, sometimes unconsciously.[12] Few men willingly give up power. However, each new generation of library administrators is less autocratic and more democratic than the preceding one. The articulate young activists now entering the profession may speed the process of change.

A young profession ought to be able to count on counsel and support from its professional association, yet the American Library Association for a great many years helped very little in the effort to win faculty status for college and university librarians. Perhaps ALA leaders did not perceive a problem, or perhaps public library interests were dominant until very recent times. Perhaps ALA was too bureaucratic, or did not believe that it should be concerned with the welfare of librarians but only with libraries. Indeed, some actions of ALA were actually harmful to academic librarians—witness the classification and pay plans of 1927, and the ready acceptance of the B.A. in Library Science as the proper degree for a fifth year of study, following the Williamson report. ALA also lacked interest in research, tended to stress unorganized education (public libraries) over organized education (academic libraries); its lack of interest in or action on basic social problems also helped no one. It is true that, indirectly, ALA was helpful in many ways. But one can speculate that academic librarians would have been much further along if they had established their own independent association, affiliated with ALA.

This lack of general acceptance and support from the professional association tended to place the burden for securing faculty status for librarians on an institutional basis. That is, each single library staff had to fight its own fight. This institutional approach frequently was quite slow, requiring two to twelve years or more. Library staffs varied in initiative and ability to conduct such a campaign. Most staffs could draw only upon the experience of other institutions for guidelines. One library tried five times before it succeeded. Many were compelled to adopt a piecemeal approach, seeking faculty rights and privileges one by one. Incidentally, few ever reported failure or the reasons therefor.

For college librarians, a special handicap was the emphasis placed by regional accrediting associations on the percentage of doctorates held by the faculty. Counting librarians as faculty usually would reduce the percentage. Therefore, some college administrators tended to oppose faculty status for librarians for this reason.

One peculiar liability was the belief of certain chief librarians that academic librarianship was a true profession but that it was different and should and could stand apart from the faculty, as an independent, equal, professional group within the university. Major proponents of this approach were E. W. McDiarmid, Donald Coney, and Lawrence Clark Powell. This proved to be a false path because the number of professional librarians in a university is very small, averaging perhaps three percent of the total faculty. This number just is not large enough or powerful enough to stand alone amidst the intense pressures and competition within the large university. Librarians must either join the faculty, or be permanently relegated to peripheral and inferior roles.

Concluding this long list of possible handicaps or liabilities is one that came into prominence after 1940. This was the establishment of State Boards of Higher Education which sometimes opposed faculty status for librarians. State legislatures, under increasing pressures for public moneys for highways in the 1920s, and from public schools and social welfare programs from the 1930s on, and from higher education, tended to establish Boards of Higher Education to evaluate and advise and perhaps to save money by coordination. The numbers of such boards increased rapidly following the appointment of the first coordinating or superimposed board by Oklahoma in 1941, simply because a superimposed board can be put in without a major overhaul of the existing institutional boards. Most states now have state-wide controlling boards.[13]

These boards have neither loyal alumni nor any other traditional means of support and defense. It is not always easy to determine if they work for the legislature or for the state institutions of higher education. But in their search for their proper role, these boards always study costs and have tended to move into the domain of staffing. Faculty are always more or less outside of their control. Thus, when librarians seek to join the faculty, this tends to raise costs and reduce the domain of the board; therefore, there is a tendency for such boards to oppose the movement. Many boards are neutral; some favor action (such as Oregon and New York). But a number of state boards of higher education have resisted the trend, notably California, or actually attacked faculty status already held by academic librarians in the system. This was the case in Florida, Pennsylvania, and New Jersey. State civil service boards occasionally oppose or attack faculty status for librarians—the Oregon system was vigorously attacked twice in forty years.

THE PATH TO THE PRESENT

Beginning with so many handicaps, academic librarianship clearly had a very difficult task ahead if it was to become a true, recognized profession. Early college and university librarianship lacked most of the characteristics of a profession so that its chances looked slim. However, a number of varied forces began to operate that were favorable to the new field.

A few early leaders, men of vision and enthusiasm, had pointed out the high-level role that librarians should have in a well-rounded educational program. Librarians were not sufficiently qualified to be able to follow their advice, but the inspirational influence of these men was not lost. The goal had been proposed.

The growing rate of publication—an "information explosion" after World War II—along with the accompanying rapid growth of collections began to require specialists in librarianship able to cope with the problems arising from this expansion of recorded knowledge. No longer could a faculty member understand or handle such an increasingly complex operation in his spare time, nor could poorly educated librarians cope with the flood and provide the quality of library services required by the college or university. Growing size, therefore, required improvement and specialization.

Newer attitudes toward the use of library resources in teaching began to emerge and be accepted.[14] These were in line with proposals of the early leaders, but were slow in gaining widespread acceptance. Leon Carnovsky's concept that "a book has no value as a social document unless it is read" expressed the newer attitude of librarians. Thus the conservation function, prominent when the rate of publication was low and collections were small, gradually lost its primacy over the utilization concept. Newer methods of teaching that called for library use to supplement the traditional classroom lecture slowly came into use by the faculty. Progress was slow but steady.

Rapidly increasing graduate study and research in universities[15] made intensive demands on the library. This was a major factor in improving the quality of library services. Research requires extensive collections and special knowledge of subject fields, book markets, and bibliography. It also demands specialized subject knowledge in library service, allied with sound bibliographic skills. Thus, graduate programs forced libraries to seek staffs better able to provide many different kinds of bibliographic services. This movement began with the first true graduate school and doctoral programs at Johns Hopkins in 1876, picked up speed from 1900 through the 1930s, and accelerated still further after World War II.

Improved library education also contributed to the movement as library schools began to provide better-educated graduates who could come closer to meeting the needs of teaching and research. Library schools were chaotic and uneven from their earliest days to the famous Williamson report of 1923 on library schools. Reforms ensued, including the raising of standards, improvement of curricula, and the establishment by ALA of the Board of Education for Librarianship, a special committee to evaluate and accredit library schools. However, even greater reforms were needed. They came in the 1940s with the overhaul and modernization of curricula, the change from the bachelor's degree to the requirement of a master's degree, and the establishment of several more doctoral programs at leading universities. Further reforms are still needed, to accommodate new theories and principles of information and communication. Some progress is being made. Curiously, despite the beginning of many new doctoral-level schools, the actual number of graduates lags dangerously behind the needs of the academic library profession.

The Graduate Library School at the University of Chicago proved to be a powerful factor in improving the status of the professional librarian.[16] It was the first doctoral-level school and the only one for a dozen years. Founded in 1928 with the encouragement and financial support of the Carnegie Corporation, it assembled a remarkable cadre of teachers, stressed research into library, bibliographic and information problems, fostered the study of libraries in their social setting, and began the profession's first scholarly journal, *The Library Quarterly*. Much of its success was due to its timeliness and to the quality of its early leaders, George A. Works and, particularly, Louis R. Wilson.

The Carnegie Corporation exerted a benevolent and important influence on the young profession, perhaps a considerably greater influence at a critical period than did the librarians' own American Library Association. The corporation saw the need to improve library education, supported the Williamson study, and actively worked to implement its recommendations. In the 1920s and 1930s, it commissioned influential studies of college libraries by William M. Randall and Harvie Branscomb. It developed standards for college library collections, then made sizable grants for development of collections first to four-year colleges and then to junior colleges. The booklists prepared by Gourlay, Mohrhardt, and Shaw were by-products. A few librarianships also were endowed. These standards and booklists, backed up by dollar grants, commanded the attention of presidents, faculty, and librarians, and helped improve general understanding of the proper public role of the college library everywhere. One of its greatest benefits was the founding of the Graduate Library School.[17] The Rosenwald Foundation and, later, the Ford Foundation lent further dimensions to library philanthropy.

Accrediting associations also lent their weight to the improvement of library service, and sometimes took positive stands on behalf of academic status for professional librarians. All regional accrediting associations include libraries as factors to be evaluated, and several have codified specific standards. In its 1947 standards, the Southern Association of Colleges and Secondary Schools recommended academic status for the librarian and his professional assistants.[18] However, the Northwest Association of Secondary and Higher Schools in 1946, and the North Central Association of Colleges and Secondary Schools in its 1952 *Manual* made such recommendations only for the head librarian.[19] Most regional accrediting associations have now moved towards general rather than specific standards, but their earlier recommendations were very helpful.

Cooperative developments in the library profession probably have exerted some influence on the respect accorded academic librarians by scholars, though these products are not widely known. A few examples are the *Union List of Serials* (1927), regional and national union catalogs, and the Farmington Plan.

The tremendous growth in the size of universities, beginning in the Depression '30s and accelerating after World War II, brought strong pressures upon academic librarians. Growing enrollments led to expanded programs in graduate study and research, which sooner or later required improved library services and led ultimately to the development of subject-specialist librarians. The inadequacies of a general university library for undergraduates led to the rise of subject divisional libraries in the late 1930s and later to separate educational units, special undergraduate libraries.

Another by-product of the growing size of universities was the steady improvement in university management tools. One of these had a very definite impact on libraries: the emergence of central personnel offices from 1950 on, to cope with the hundreds or, indeed, thousands of nonacademic employees. When these offices were organized, the vague status of librarians in many institutions came to light, and the issue was forced—librarians ultimately were recognized as faculty, or assigned to classified groups along with accountants, secretaries, janitors, and the dozens of other classifications, under the control of the personnel office. Thus the advent of the university personnel office forced the issue and often accelerated the movement towards faculty status for librarians.

A few early classic works, mostly of the 1930s and early 1940s, focused attention on educational and research factors in the academic library world, and indicated the growing maturity of academic librarians. Among these might be mentioned George A. Works', *College and University Library Problems* (1927); Louis R. Wilson's *Geography of Reading* (1938), and with Maurice Tauber, his first great textbook on *The University Library* (1945); R. B. Downs' *Resources of Southern Libraries* (1938) and *Union Catalogs in the United States* (1942); Harvie Branscomb's *Teaching with Books* (1940); Wilhelm Munthe's *American Librarianship from a European Angle* (1939); Guy R. Lyle's first real textbook on the college library, *Administration of the College Library* (1944); and Fremont Rider's *The Scholar and the Future of the Research Library* (1944). To these were added the persistent influence of certain leaders active from the 1940s on in the campaign to achieve academic recognition, such as William H. Carlson, Ralph Ellsworth, Frank Lundy, and R. B. Downs. Downs was the first director of a very large university library to secure academic status for his professional staff, and has been active ever since, promoting faculty status through his speaking and writing and by activities in professional associations.

College and Research Libraries, founded in 1939 as the organ of the Association of College and Research Libraries, has proved very influential as a forum and a vehicle for the dissemination of ideas. Most of the articles on the educational role of academic libraries and on faculty status for their librarians have appeared in its pages. It has always contained some excellent articles, and its quality has increased steadily over the years.

The Association of Research Libraries, organized in 1932, also has contributed to the status and prestige of academic librarianship. Limited in membership to chief librarians of the larger research libraries, it can focus on major problems and has been singularly effective in securing action. Its influence has been exerted more on other professional problems, personnel, and matters, however, but it has helped improve the caliber of university librarianship.

The action of the American Association of University Professors in welcoming professional academic librarians into membership, in 1956, was helpful indeed in fostering faculty consent and approval. In that year its Council ruled that "librarians of professional status are engaged in teaching and research" and opened its doors under certain conditions. The librarian had to be in an eligible institution and have the status of a member of the faculty with the rank of instructor or its equivalent. Some 738 librarians had joined AAUP by 1957.[20] The current rule is "should a librarian . . . hold faculty status and rank and have the right to vote at faculty senate meetings, then he is eligible for active membership."[21] By 1967, younger librarians seemed to find membership in the AAUP increasingly attractive in comparison with membership in ALA.[22] Labor unions as an alternative to ALA—the ACRL or the AAUP have an appeal to some. In those institutions in which the classroom faculty have chosen to organize as a labor union, librarians have been welcomed and have joined.

A most influential professional group in the drive for academic recognition for librarians was the Committee on Academic Status of the University Libraries Section of ACRL. This committee was established in 1958 at the urging of R. B. Downs, a leader in the movement, who saw the need for a formal body to carry on some of the work previously done on an individual basis. Under the chairmanship of Arthur McAnally, it was the first ALA body to officially and formally endorse faculty status as a policy and a right, in 1959, and this statement was approved by ACRL and ALA.[23] Then the committee set out to discover facts, specify principles, spell out details, and marshal arguments. More than a dozen articles were produced by members, on assignment, over the next ten years. Authors included R. B. Downs (three items), Arthur McAnally (two), William H. Jesse, Lewis C. Branscomb, W. Porter Kellam, and Carl W. Hintz. Subjects dealt with were the privileges and obligations of academic status, procedures in seeking status, a survey of conditions, a history of the movement, professional duties in libraries, staff opportunities for study and research, full participation in the educational enterprise, criteria for appointment and promotion, and tenure matters. Thus the work of this committee represented a very important stage in the movement, establishing overall policies and spelling out details for the guidance of the profession. It also engaged in promotional and supportive work with libraries. In 1969 it was converted to a general committee of the entire ACRL.

Finally, at the Atlantic City Conference of ALA in 1969, a large number of young activists in academic libraries, strongly concerned about current social problems, irritated at the slow and often-delayed movement toward faculty status for all, and dismayed at ALA inactivity, led a putsch in ACRL, which finally convinced ALA that it must reconsider its traditional attitude of support for libraries rather than for librarians. This may lead in time to a thoroughgoing reorientation and reorganization of ALA itself. As one result, ACRL acknowledged a responsibility for active support of faculty status for academic librarians, resolved to attempt to enforce it by whatever means possible, and secured the reluctant support of ALA itself for the principle and the action.

It has now been nearly a century since faculty status for professional librarians was first proposed. Progress has been slow and irregular because of the aforementioned reasons. The profession has had to grow up. Recognition of the need has had to develop, and efforts have had to be made institution by institution. But the course of events has brought faculty status of one kind or another to the majority of academic librarians, though certainly not to all.[24] There is great variety still in the types of academic status held by librarians. Too many librarians are at the instructor level. Salaries are still below the classroom faculty average in the great majority of institutions, though we have come a long way from 1939 when a visitor could say caustically that librarianship was the worst-paid profession in the United States and obviously based on the idea of celibacy.[25] Most librarians still have twelve-month contracts. Research is inadequate, there are far too few doctorates, and vision and innovation are seldom seen. Even after faculty status is secured, some colleges and universities have had to weather attacks on their librarians, usually from state agencies outside the institution. This has occurred in Oregon, Pennsylvania, Florida, and New Jersey. Faculty status is not yet fully accepted. However, academic librarians now have the endorsement and active support of their professional association.

FUTURE EVOLUTION OF FACULTY STATUS

The long-term consequences of faculty status for professional librarians in colleges and universities can be perceived only dimly at present. Most future developments clearly will be evolutionary. However, the implications in some areas such as library management are revolutionary.

National Acceptance Near

Faculty status for academic librarians and library specialists is now accepted rather generally as appropriate and advantageous. The majority of college and university librarians already have this recognition in some form. The trend is well-established and continuing so that nationwide acceptance probably is near. Not too far in the future, those institutions that do not offer such status may be regarded as oddities.

Educational Role of Libraries

One of the most important results of faculty status for librarians is likely to be a gradual change in the educational role of the library within the institution. Two factors may be responsible: the growing capabilities and interest of the library faculty in educational affairs, and the student revolution which began rather simply with the Free Speech Movement at Berkeley in 1964 but now has been enlarged in scope to a basic questioning of long-established educational practices all across the country. Students demand more relevance, greater freedom, and more opportunity for individual learning. Any educational program that places more responsibility on the student for his own education necessarily involves greater use of books and libraries. Compulsory class attendance is being questioned severely, as is the traditional compartmentalized curriculum. What may emerge ultimately no one knows.[26] It is to be hoped that if changes are made, the personalized Oxford–Cambridge method may be the pattern, rather than the political orientation of the South American University. The movement certainly does have similarities to the great "University Reform" movement that swept South America after 1919. Whatever the outcome, changes seem to be in the wind. Librarians may not be ready yet to participate fully in new-style colleges and experimental educational plans, but possessing faculty status librarians are in a better position now than ever before to fulfill their responsibilities to such new plans.[27]

Government and Administration

Sweeping changes are likely in library government and administration. When librarians obtain faculty status, then they actually become a faculty. So far, few library administrators have realized exactly what this implies. A faculty, be it a department, school, or college, is an association of colleagues banded together by a common interest. They establish their own policies concerning themselves and their work, within limits, and conduct their own affairs. They usually vote, or a subcommittee does, on new appointments, promotions, and tenure recommendations. They accept leadership but they tend to resent authority and to reject dictators.

They are not administered though they may be led; they are co-equals, colleagues, and individualists.

As librarians realize that they are a faculty, and begin to look at other faculties, they will find operation as a faculty satisfying and desirable. They will expect similar participation in library affairs. Therefore, the traditional hierarchical structure of large academic libraries, insofar as it relates to professional librarians and specialists, will undoubtedly be modified. Increasing activism in the younger staff is already evident. The chief librarian in a university probably will become less a line officer administrator, and more a leader or persuader, much like a dean.[28]

Smaller academic staffs are likely to operate as a department, or an undivided college in a university. Larger university library staffs are likely to operate as a large college, with the director in the position of a dean, and to contain several departments in the college. The first split is likely to be into departments of readers' services and technical services. Very large staffs may well add departments of branch libraries, or split up technical services, or make other such divisions. Regular faculty meetings will be necessary—most universities require that a faculty meet once a month. Traditional departments usually can conduct their business within an hour or so a month; library faculties will require more time until they shake down to a routine. Classroom faculties regard these meetings as essential and find time for them; librarians are going to have to do likewise. Clearly more committees will be used, for the committee is the means through which a faculty exercises its duties and rights in government and administration. Greater participation of the library staff in policy decisions and the setting of goals is to be expected.

A word of caution is in order. At least two librarians have voiced concern over whether or not staff operation as a library faculty is practicable. Donald Coney has said that it remained to be seen how far the library could go in allowing staff participation in policy decisions.[29] Stuart Forth has pointed out that the university library serves all parts of the university; its success or failure affects all departments. A traditional department affects only itself, not the entire university. So he asked, can the university afford to permit the library staff to run the library?[30] However, Bundy and Wasserman in a very carefully reasoned paper write that the present organizational structure of university libraries inhibits the flow of ideas, and tends to preserve the status quo at any cost, even though change may be of fundamental importance. ". . . It is essential for professionals in organizations to assume decision-making responsibilities in relation to goals and standards of service. Yet, with only rare exceptions, libraries fall into that class of organizations in which goal decisions are tightly controlled by the administrative hierarchy. They are, consequently, often at the mercy of other tendencies of bureaucracy which run counter to professional aspirations and responsibilities."[31] They consider the movement in the direction of greater staff participation a growing-up of the profession and vital to the future progress of academic librarianship. Otherwise, in the world of information, the academic librarian may soon be suspended and relegated to a negligible role.

Only a handful of university library staffs have begun to try to operate as a faculty. These include Cornell, Oregon, Houston, Penn State, and Oklahoma. All are feeling their way, but the system appears to work, and all continue to move forward.

Tenure of Chairmen, Directors, and Deans

In many democratically governed universities, a department is presided over by a chairman whose tenure is for a limited term, often four years. Usually he may be reappointed with the consent of his faculty and of the administration. The older traditional pattern is to have department heads whose tenure is permanent or indefinite. In both kinds of organization, however, deans usually are permanent appointments. Even in those institutions such as Illinois, where a review of a dean's tenure is specified every fifth year, the dean usually is continued in office as a routine matter unless objections come to light. The director of a university library corresponds more closely to a dean than to any other academic officer. The question of rotating department chairmanships, however, is likely to be raised sooner or later in large university libraries.

Advisory Committees versus Department Head Meetings

Librarians operating as a faculty are suspicious of weekly or monthly Department Head meetings. They suspect that decisions may be made in such meetings on policies and other matters which affect them and which they feel are rightly within their own province. However, inviting in nonadministrative personnel regularly—persons who have special knowledge on the topic or topics to be discussed—apparently allays these suspicions.

An advisory, or "executive," committee to a chairman and a dean is common in those institutions in which the faculty have a major role in government and administration. (It has been said that a high degree of faculty participation is one of the earmarks of a high-quality institution— a strong faculty requires it.) In any event, such an advisory committee of the library faculty seems to function well and also to be quite pleasing to the library faculty. The division of responsibilities, corresponding to classroom faculty practices, is often as follows. The faculty as a whole deals with major policies, goals and standards, appointments to the faculty, and recommendations regarding tenure. The advisory committee may deal with salary raises, promotions in rank, budget, and occasional problems and procedures.[32] Such a committee is no substitute for the regular monthly faculty meeting, of course, but operates in a clearly defined sphere and can serve as a substitute for faculty opinion and action during intervals between monthly faculty meetings.

The Administrative Dichotomy

In the modern university library, the professional staff is composed, increasingly, of two separate and distinct groups: specialists and administrators. The rise of the specialist in subject, language, area, etc., and of archivists, curators, media specialists, and systems analysts, has been commented on frequently in library literature. Specialists in a university are no longer a subordinate level of workers, but colleagues who evaluate themselves and determine educational policy. They are not in the hierarchical organization structure of the university.[33] Library specialists are essential if one is to give good service to graduate students, to faculty, and to highly specialized research projects. They are, in fact, fully as important to the university as is the library administrator. Note, as a parallel, that distinguished professors in good universities often receive salaries equal to those of deans.

Administrative accomplishment tends to be given a higher value than professional practice in a bureaucracy, yet Bundy and Wasserman point out that time spent in administrative work is also time spent in nonprofessional practice.[34] It is an observable fact that when a classroom faculty member leaves the classroom for administration, he may try to keep up with his discipline for a time and try to do some teaching but soon finds the second task impossible. Thus, administrative work tends to be detrimental to scholarship and professional activity.

Vosper proposed to separate career ladders in the university library, one for the administrator, and a second for the subject specialist. Each ladder should lead to the same heights.[35] This may well be the way it will be. To the writer, this situation represents a dilemma: Are library science doctorates to be only administrators and are all other staff to have subject doctorates in time? What will be their common meeting ground? Whatever the ultimate outcome, clearly the subject (or other) specialist should be able to advance in rank and salary at the same pace and to the same levels as the library administrator. In a classroom department, a man of ability can advance from instructor to full professor without ever assuming any administrative duties. Certainly the same possibility must be open to library faculties. This problem is not so evident in college libraries, of course.

Size of Departments

If the library staff is to operate as a faculty, then library departments must be large enough to permit members to take classes, have time off for research projects, take sabbatical leaves, and be absent for other good causes. One-to-three-man units are just too small and will have to be consolidated. In answer to the contention that the absence of the library specialist may be critical, it may be said that it is no more critical than the absence on leave of the specialist in Restoration drama in English, or the cactus and succulent plant specialist in botany. Accommodations can be made.

Academic Freedom and Tenure

One of the major values of faculty status is the right to academic freedom, essential to the pursuit of truth. Tenure protects academic freedom and is an essential corollary. The "1940 Statement of Principles in Academic Freedom and Tenure" formulated by the American Association of University Professors is the classic statement on this subject.[36] These principles were adapted to libraries and then adopted by the American

Library Association.[37] However, while the library adaptation is good, its tenure statement is inferior to that of the AAUP, since the Council adopted the weaker of two proposed drafts. Academic librarians should use the AAUP statement.

Until very recently, librarians have not been keenly interested in academic freedom, except as the basis for tenure. As recently as 1968, one librarian could truthfully write that "Academic librarians have not notably participated vigorously and publicly in the broad citizen movements of our time in contrast to the often very effective efforts by their colleagues on the faculty. . . . One of the problems in the extension of tenure to the academic librarian lies in the reluctance of both faculty members and librarians themselves to accept the need for the responsibilities and rights implicit in the concept of tenure."[38] However, the pent-up eruptions of the young at the Atlantic City Conference of ALA in 1969, and the recent actions of the FBI investigating reading records in Atlanta and at Wisconsin indicate that conditions have changed indeed. Actually, librarians began to be concerned about attacks on intellectual freedom as far back as the 1940s.[39]

Three aspects of librarianship are involved in academic–intellectual freedom: (1) freedom of the library to select, maintain, and provide materials on any subject from any viewpoint, whether or not controversial, unpopular, or seemingly absolutely wrong; (2) the right of students and faculty to have access to these materials and to use them in privacy; (3) protection for the librarian who selects and provides and promotes use of library materials.

Recommendations for tenure is one of the most important actions of any faculty, for this is the device by which the group assures the maintenance of the quality of its membership. Universities and colleges are usually definite in specifying qualifications for tenure and very specific in outlining procedures for the granting of tenure. Bases for the abrogation of tenure are spelled out, and procedures for appeal are always stated. The entire faculty of a department usually votes on the granting of tenure, though frequently only those who already hold tenure may vote. A good statement of the reasons libraries need tenure has been developed but may need updating.[40] Regulations vary somewhat from institution to institution, though they usually conform closely to the recommendations of AAUP. Of course librarians must be governed by the faculty regulations on tenure of their respective institutions. It should be mentioned that the principles of academic freedom and tenure have been under attack recently, as a result of student disturbances on campus. If this is lost, then higher education will be in serious danger.

Peer Evaluation

One of the prerogatives of professional and collegial (i.e., as colleagues) organizations, such as a faculty, is the right of a member to be judged by his peers. Only a colleague can fairly evaluate a man's true capabilities and performance. Therefore, faculty members insist on evaluation by their own kind in matters of appointment, promotion, and tenure. This principle is usually, but not always, extended to salary increases. Appointment and tenure are voted on by the entire faculty or tenured faculty, while promotions in rank usually are passed on by an elected committee of the faculty. This committee usually makes the initial or basic recommendations on increases in salary. Of course, all of these recommendations must be approved in turn by the academic administration. This applies only to positive recommendations; negative recommendations are final and do not proceed further.

Librarians and library administrators must begin to accept these principles and practices. Some library administrators may mistrust the judgment of their staffs for a time. However, library faculty tend to be pretty hard-nosed in their peer judgments; also, the administrator has the right to concur or dissent, with both recommendations usually passed on up the line. Thus, he does not give up all authority provided he has the confidence of the university administration, but under this system he must be prepared to justify his decisions and cannot act arbitrarily or autocratically. Department heads and deans usually do not have the final decision in such matters, this being reserved for the Provost or President. But if they do, chief librarians should consider every action carefully rather than oppose their faculty frequently and possibly lose their confidence or alienate the entire group. The quality of a faculty has to be good before this democratic system will be successful; a weak department tends to perpetuate weakness in choosing new members, granting tenure, approving promotions, and awarding salary increases. The administration of a college or university finds it difficult to intervene and improve quality in a poor department, but there are ways. One of the first is to replace the head of the unit.

Criteria for faculty appointment, promotion, tenure, and salary increases usually are well defined in a good college or university, and should apply to a library faculty as well. The three principal criteria are success in teaching, research performed, and services performed. Some institutions split these into four, five, or six elements, but all derive from these three. A candidate usually must qualify on two of the three factors. Certain adaptations or interpretations are necessary to cover librarians. These adaptations have already been outlined in general terms.[41] A number of university libraries have developed detailed statements concerning criteria for librarians holding faculty status, some in great detail, such as Ohio State, Oregon, Idaho, Cornell, and Oklahoma.[42]

The Work Week and the Contract Year

Classroom faculty members must meet some specific weekly schedules, but these amount to only a few hours per week. The rest of their work is not done on schedule—including preparation for classes, grading, reading to keep up in the field, etc. If a faculty member teaches nine hours, then he may be expected to devote two hours for each class hour to preparation, grading papers, etc. He also is expected to maintain some office hours for consultation with students, perhaps three hours per week. Thus, the more or less compulsory time expended in doing his basic job is nine hours plus eighteen hours plus three hours for a total of thirty hours per week. The remainder of a standard work week of forty hours he is expected to devote to research committee service, and similar duties.

Academic librarianship is a very fast-moving field, as it attempts to cope with the evergrowing flood of knowledge and provide the specialized services demanded by faculty and students. The profession desperately needs research, and each library also needs high-level administrative studies related to that particular library. Librarians also need to keep up with the rapid developments that are taking place. They must also have time for self-improvement, especially the subject specialist group. Therefore, librarians operating at a faculty level should have some unscheduled time each week for reading and research. It is recognized that librarians engaged in extended research projects, just as faculty, must carry on the work partly as overload or on leave. A librarian working on an extensive administrative study directed toward solving a problem in his library should be relieved of other duties while thus occupied. Sabbatical leaves are essential, of course, but not suitable for all purposes.

In time, the work-week principles of the University of Oregon Library probably will be accepted throughout the profession. That Library probably states that there is no specified work week, but that each professional librarian is a responsible person and expected to do the work assigned to him. If doing his duty requires more than forty hours per week, then the library administration is at fault and should correct the staffing or the assignment. The recent action of the California State College librarians in announcing that they had to have ten hours a week, unscheduled, to fulfill academic and professional responsibilities, and then proceeding to take this time, is worthy of note. It seems likely that within a few years the "scheduled work week" will be thirty hours, with ten additional hours expected to be used for professional improvement, taking classes in a specialty, research, committee work, service to the profession, etc. Those who abuse this privilege are not of academic caliber and unworthy of continued employment. The library faculty themselves probably will police their privileges thoroughly, to prevent abuse, and to protect their rights to status. This plan should improve, greatly, the quality of service to the institution and be well worth the cost. Supporting staff will have to be used more extensively.

The contract year for librarians may be either twelve months or nine months. The first is far more common for librarians, but the latter for classroom faculty. Some college faculties (education, for example) are often on twelve-month contracts, as are department chairmen in universities. Nine-month contracts for librarians are more desirable, with extra pay if they work during the summer session. If twelve-month contracts are used, the salary should be adjusted. Leaves during the summer should be permissible; vacations should be one month; and at least half of the Thanksgiving, Easter, and Christmas holidays for classroom faculty should be authorized for librarians. Unfortunately for librarians, some faculty, graduate students and undergraduate students often remain on campus during holidays and use the library so that minimum schedules must be maintained.

Library administrators sometimes oppose nine-month contracts for professional librarians primarily because it would mean more work for them. Also the college or university administration may find the added cost difficult to absorb. However, the advantages to the staff are obvious. Institutions do manage to cope with the summer session problem successfully and there is no reason that libraries cannot do as well. This privilege might be the next-to-last faculty prerogative gained by librarians—comparable salaries might be last—but its acceptance in the future appears inevitable. It is professionally beneficial to take the summer off for professional development; it is also good for the institution. The librarians want it and, becoming more cohesive and vocal, will demand it. The contract year also has a bearing on salaries. Staff pressure for approval, therefore, may be maintained. Incidentally, some rules about shifting back and forth from nine to twelve months may be required.

Faculty Meetings

Departments and colleges usually carry on their business in monthly meetings, whereas general faculties may meet only once or twice a year. Details and special problems are dealt with by standing and ad hoc committees. Library faculties will follow institutional policies. Minutes of meetings and reports of committees should be distributed to all if the library faculty is large in numbers.

Titles and Ranks

Professional librarians should be eligible for appointment to the traditional ranks and titles of instructor, assistant professor, associate professor, and professor. The use of equivalences should be regarded as a temporary expedient. A proper distribution among ranks should be observed. However, unless quotas for each rank are set locally for all departments, they should not be set for librarians. Far too many librarians are at the instructor level at present;[43] vigorous efforts must be made to improve the distribution. However, the common five-years-up-or-out rule may need to be waived for librarians for a few years, or the special instructor title used, while some upgrading of staff is pending. As noted earlier, subject or other specialists are entitled to promotion and advancement in salary without having to change jobs or assume any administrative duties, like classroom faculty. The terminal degree at present for administrators is the master's degree, except for the chief librarian, where any college or university president logically expects the doctorate. The specialist is expected to have the professional master's degree and also to have or acquire a master's degree in the subject. In time, and this may take a long time, a doctor's degree probably will be required for both groups. The administrator's is likely to be in library science, the specialist's in his special field. The doctorate probably will be necessary because of the growing complexities of academic librarianship and for survival.

Continuing Education and Professional Growth

"While there may be terminal academic degrees, there never can be an end to the continued learning which alone insures against inflexibility in the face of new problems."[44] In addition, the growing demand in colleges, and especially universities, for specialists in subjects, languages, areas, and forms of material also requires that librarians be permitted and encouraged to pursue advanced degrees. Library schools do not produce many such specialists; usually the library has to develop its own. Schiller found one librarian in eight currently enrolled for credit towards an advanced degree.[45] Provisions required to encourage and facilitate this activity are a suitable work week, nine-month contracts or educational leave with pay, and sabbatical leaves. Many universities have rules against a faculty member above the rank of instructor pursuing a degree locally, for obvious reasons. Waivers will have to be sought for professional librarians because of the dual requirements laid upon them by the university for competence in both a profession and a specialty. It is in the university's interest to find the means. A most thorough attempt to examine systematically the problems and possibilities of continuing education and professional growth in a large university library was that undertaken at Cornell in 1968–1969.[46] William H. Jesse also surveyed practices for the Committee on Academic Status of ACRL, and developed proposed policies.[47]

Supporting Staff

In any library, there is a multitude of subprofessional, routine, and clerical tasks that do not require professional training and ability. These must be performed by a supporting staff of subprofessional and clerical assistants. The proportion of supporting staff to librarians should be at least two to one; in large libraries, probably three to one or four to one.[48] Librarians performing clerical tasks are not entitled to faculty status.

As recently as 1950, the library staffs of many, if not most, college and university libraries of the country consisted of fifty to ninety percent "professional" librarians. However, after the initial airing of this most unsatisfactory condition by George A. Works in 1927, many writers have commented on the problem and urged correction: Donald Coney, Melvin Voigt, Archie McNeal, Paul Wasserman, R. B. Downs, among others. The logic and need of a better distribution was recognized long ago and adjustments have been made nearly everywhere. Currently, machines are being used, increasingly, for routine and repetitive tasks that are amenable to machine handling; this trend will unquestionably accelerate. These are both highly desirable developments, of course.

The role of this supporting staff is quite important, is likely to become considerably larger in the future, and needs to be reexamined thoroughly. Many of these jobs are sadly lacking in responsibility and variety. A dilemma has arisen as faculty status has been secured by the professional staff: the organization of library faculty leaves out the supporting staff, yet they do most of the work in a library, and they outnumber the professional staff considerably. It seems essential that the library administration recognize their needs and interests fully and give far more attention to this group.[49] Indeed, the supporting staff and other library administrative personnel may become the principal concerns of chief librarians for several years until this problem is resolved. Unionization is one alternative.[50]

Size and Quality of Staff

"Academic libraries do not need a great many additional professionals. If anything, we have too many librarians now: most of them spend the bulk of their time doing clerical work which non-professional personnel can perform equally well for substantially less money. What academic libraries need is fewer but better educated librarians. . . ."[51] This may seem a shocking statement to many administrators. But substantiation is offered by the University of Michigan Libraries, where there has been a very substantial increase in expenditures for salaries and wages over the past ten years, most of which has gone into improvement of salaries and very little into additional staff. Similarly, at the University of Oklahoma the size of the professional staff has been almost stable for the past fifteen years, although the number of classified or supporting staff has almost tripled. The bureaucratic attitude towards growth needs to be reexamined critically. It is true that many libraries were inadequately staffed fifteen years ago, ten years ago, and some are even now. But perhaps the profession needs higher quality rather than an increase in quantity. The classroom faculty at most institutions has not grown in size as rapidly as has enrollment—large lecture sections, greater use of teaching assistants, and other such devices have been used, though currently all these practices tend to be questioned by students. In any case, standards for professional staffing, especially in universities, are needed.

Joint Appointments

Libraries might explore, with profit, joint appointments with classroom departments, especially in the bibliographer reference–curator field. They tend to promote coordination as well as understanding and are beneficial to both organizations. The University of Oklahoma Library has had five of these, some dating back for twenty years, and has found them interesting and practicable.

The Faculty Library Committee

Faculty status for librarians brings into question the traditional role of the faculty library committee. This committee is a representative group of the classroom faculty who advise on policies and help interpret the library to the faculty and faculty interests and needs to the library. One of its principal concerns has always been book funds. Recently, student members have been added to many such committees. Munthe, comparing the American university and the European as a foreign observer, was quite critical of certain aspects of the faculty library committee. He saw it as detrimental to the welfare of the library in that it tends to preserve "the outmoded system, which is still found in some universities, of parcelling out the (book) funds by departments of instruction."[52] He regarded development of collections, properly, as the province of librarians as it is in European universities. It is interesting to note that some large university libraries such as Indiana have begun to move in the direction of the European practice, using subject-specialist bibliographers. The growing number and capabilities of subject specialists in university libraries will make this an issue. Criticisms of faculty selection go as far back as the thirties in studies by William M. Randall, Ralph E. Ellsworth, Munthe, and others. Recently, the evergrowing pressures on the classroom faculty tend to make them welcome relief from the chore of book selection. Domestic all-books approval plans usually are welcomed enthusiastically. The Farmington Plan and approval plans for British, European, and Latin American publications seem to be accepted widely.[53] This movement probably will accelerate.

Research and Innovation

The continued success and, indeed, the survival of the academic library as such may depend on the ability of the library to cope with new ideas and problems in the rapidly expanding world of information resources. Research and innovation are of vital importance. Research is also one of the traditional measures of faculty competence—indeed, the only tangible evidence of originality, continuing scholarly interest, and professional dedication. Hopefully, research also may advance the discipline through the discovery of new knowledge. Most library administrators are much in favor of research by the library staff, and library faculty members are beginning to struggle with the problem.[54] Numerous obstacles still exist. In time there may be no place in the university library for the librarian who is not interested in research.

Innovation is an acute problem because of its relative absence. Bureaucracy tends to oppose innovation; library schools do not teach innovative attitudes; the profession is still struggling to reach a respectable level of research activity. Yet the world of information and its dissemination is in ferment.[55] One interesting suggestion is that academic librarians look to information science as the source of new ideas.[56]

The Problems of Captives and Sex

Schiller found that between seven and eight percent of academic librarians were married to a classroom faculty member. About three fourths of them were faculty wives. While their professional qualifications often equalled or exceeded those of others, several of the women commented that nepotism had been a barrier to advancement in their library careers.[57] The employment of such persons on the basis of simple availability or because they can be hired cheaply, qualified though they may be, seems unwise from the viewpoint of the library faculty as a whole. It is not just, but they tend to be discriminated against in salary and other matters, consciously or unconsciously, and their employment therefore tends to hold down the salaries of the rest of the staff. Classroom faculty do not usually employ regular faculty members on any such basis. Perhaps emergency employment, such as visiting or special lectures, might reduce the problem.

The sex distribution in academic libraries unfortunately tends to militate against acceptance of librarians as colleagues by the faculty. Again this is neither fair nor just. Attitudes of all faculty probably would be more favorable toward librarians if the percentage of men in librarianship were higher or even corresponded to the percentage distribution among the faculty as a whole. However, the academic library profession is never likely to have more men than women. If present trends continue —a steady increase in the percentage of academic librarians who are male—then an equal balance ultimately may result. Perhaps the present distribution among classroom faculties—that is, eighty percent male and twenty percent female—also will change.

Educational Variety

Librarians for any staff should be recruited from different universities, to secure the values of variety in background and approaches. This is standard faculty practice. A recent survey indicates that those university libraries where there are accredited library schools are very heavily overloaded with local graduates.[58] The local school may be one of the best, but it is educationally unsound to have too many graduates from any one school. No respectable classroom faculty would tolerate such maldistribution. Variety in background is stimulating and gives differing viewpoints.

However, subject and other specialist librarians are likely to have to secure advanced degrees in their specialty locally. There are just not enough qualified specialists produced by the library schools at present to meet the need, and most have to continue their special education after appointment. This situation is one of necessity at present, but should not be permanent. So long as part of the academic qualifications are earned elsewhere, the result may be acceptable.

Mobility

As librarians become more professionally minded and more faculty oriented, they will all discover a fact that classroom faculty have known for a long time. The fastest advancement in salary and rank comes through changing positions, moving from one library to a better position in another.[59] An AAUP study of the 1930s amply demonstrated this fact. In fact, ambitious faculty have been called humorously "migratory labor." Therefore, mobility in the profession is very likely to increase steadily, to the benefit of everyone. Schiller does note that women tend to be less mobile than men.[60] Current surpluses of doctorates in certain subjects may dampen movement for a while. It also might offer some opportunities to academic libraries to acquire specialists!

The Future Leaders

It is heartening to see the growing concern of young librarians with major social problems of our times, and their active efforts, beginning at Atlantic City in 1969, to reshape the professional associations. So many authors have commented earlier on the apathy of librarians toward educational concerns and social problems. It is a pleasure to see them— action-oriented, alert, eager, confident, and fearless. Unquestionably, they will be very influential in the movement toward faculty-level operation and full faculty status for all academic librarians. It is past time for the concerted action that they are beginning to demand.

References

1. These early stirrings are reported ably by R. B. Downs in "Status of Academic Librarians in Retrospect," *College and Research Libraries* 29 (July, 1968): 253–258. A brief earlier history is given by William H. Carlson in "The Trend Toward Academic Recognition of College Librarians," *College and Research Libraries* 16 (Jan., 1955): 24–29.
2. H. A. Sawtelle, "The College Librarianship," *Library Journal* 3 (June, 1878): 162.

3. George A. Works, *College and University Library Problems* (Chicago: American Librarianship Association, 1927), pp. 80–98.

4. See Sarah K. Vann, *Training for Librarianship before 1925* (Chicago: American Library Association, 1961). See also Gerald Bramley, *A History of Library Education* (Hamden, Conn.: Archon Books, 1969).

5. Carnegie Corporation of New York, *Training for Library Service: a Report Prepared for the Carnegie Corporation of New York*, by Charles C. Williamson (New York, 1923).

6. Mary Wright Plummer, *The Seven Joys of Reading* (White Plains, N.Y.: H. W. Wilson Co., 1916), p. 3.

7. See Florence Holbrook, "The Faculty Image of the Academic Librarian," *Southeastern Librarian* 18 (Fall, 1968): 174–193. A more optimistic view was given by R. B. Downs in "The Place of College Librarians in the Academic World," *California Librarian* 28 (Winter, 1960): 101–106.

8. Anita R. Schiller, *Characteristics of Professional Personnel in College and University Libraries* (Urbana, Ill.: Graduate School of Library Science, University of Illinois, May, 1968), p. 64.

9. Robert T. Blackburn, "College Librarians—Indicated Failures: Some Reasons and a Possible Remedy," *College and Research Libraries* 29 (May, 1968): 171–177.

10. For a good discussion of bureaucracy in the college and university, see Nicholas J. Demerath (and others), *Power, Presidents, and Professors* (New York: Basic Books, 1967). See also Herbert Stroup, *Bureaucracy in Higher Education* (New York: Free Press, 1966). For the professional's attitude towards bureaucracy, see Howard M. Vollmer and Donald L. Mills, eds., *Professionalization* (Englewood Cliffs, N.J.: Prentice-Hall, 1966). For new schools of thought in general organization theory, most of which involve greater participation by staff, see the succinct study by Timothy Hallinan, *New Directions in Organization Theory* (Santa Monica, Cal.: The RAND Corporation, Sept., 1968. RAND, P–3936).

11. See Eldred Smith, "Academic Status for College and University Librarians—Problems and Prospects," *College and Research Libraries* 31 (Jan., 1970): 10. The importance of this factor is noted also by Mary Lee Bundy and Paul Wasserman, "Professionalism Reconsidered," *College and Research Libraries* 29 (Jan., 1968): 15.

12. See Donald Coney in University of California (Berkeley) Library, "Report of the University Librarian, 1967–68," in *C. U. News* 23:3 (June 6, 1968): p. 4.

13. See John J. Corson, *Governance of College and Universities* (New York: McGraw-Hill, 1960). Also for dangers see Lyman A. Glenny, *Anatomy of Public Colleges: the Challenge of Coordination* (New York: McGraw-Hill, 1959).

14. There are dozens of articles on this subject, and a few books. Representative is Harvie Branscomb, *Teaching with Books: a Study of College Libraries* (Chicago: Association of American Colleges, American Library Association, 1940).

15. Bernard Berelson, *Graduate Education in the United States* (New York: McGraw-Hill, 1960).

16. See Wilhelm Munthe, *American Librarianship from a European Angle; an Attempt at an Evaluation of Policies and Activities* (Chicago: American Library Association, 1939), pp. 144–154. Also Kenneth J. Brough, *Scholar's Workshop; Evolving Conceptions of Library Service* (Urbana: University of Illinois Press, 1953), p. 168.

17. Carnegie Corporation of New York. *Library Program, 1911–1961,* by Florence Anderson (New York, 1963). See also Wilhelm Munthe, op. cit., pp. 99–101, and Kenneth J. Brough, op. cit., p. 168 ff.
18. Cited by William H. Carlson, "The Trend toward Academic Recognition of College Librarians," *College and Research Libraries* 16 (Jan., 1955): 24–29.
19. Association of College and Research Libraries, Committee on Standards, *College and University Library Accrediting Standards,* ed. by Eli Oboler (and others) (Chicago: A.C.R.L., 1958. A.C.R.L. Monograph no. 20), p. 12.
20. Cited in R. B. Downs, "The Current Status of University Library Staffs," *College and Research Libraries* 18 (Sept., 1957): p. 384.
21. Letter from Mrs. Virginia C. Little, Membership Development AAUP, dated March 8, 1968, quoted in University of Washington Libraries, *Report of the Ad Hoc Committee on the Status of Librarians* (Seattle, 1968), p. 19.
22. Anita R. Schiller, op. cit., pp. 54–55.
23. "Status of College and University Librarians," *College and Research Libraries* 20 (Sept., 1959): 399–400.
24. Anita R. Schiller, op. cit., p. 63 ff.
25. Wilhelm Munthe, op. cit., p. 165.
26. There are dozens of books on the subject. Representative are Jerome H. Shalnick, *Politics of Protest* (N.Y.: Simon & Schuster, 1969); and Cox Commission, *Crisis at Columbia; Report of the Fact-Finding Commission Appointed to Investigate the Disturbance at Columbia University in April and May, 1968* (New York: Random House, 1968). For a good treatment of possible educational reforms, see Christopher Jeneks and David Riesman, *The Academic Revolution* (Garden City, N.Y.: Doubleday, 1968). However, a more pessimistic view, that changes are unlikely unless the pressure is very great, is expressed by J. Lon Hefferlin, *Dynamics of Academic Reform* (San Francisco: Jossey-Bass, 1969). Further evidence of the strength of traditional patterns is revealed in an examination of new universities around the world—many begin with educational innovations, but as they gain strength they almost invariably move toward the established pattern. See Murray G. Ross, ed., *New Universities in the Modern World* (New York: St. Martin's Press, 1966).
27. A broad-gauge proposal of this kind, though limited to medical libraries, is M. K. DuVal, "Changing Role of the Library," *Bulletin of the Medical Library Association* 53 (Jan., 1968): 32–35.
28. See, for example, Arthur J. Dibden, ed., *The Academic Deanship in American Colleges and Universities* (Carbondale: Southern Illinois University Press, 1968).
29. University of California (Berkeley) Library, *Report of the University Librarian, 1967–68,* reprinted in *C.U. News* 23:3 (June 6, 1968): p. 4.
30. Statement, oral, before the ACRL Committee on Academic Status, Detroit, Mich., June 30, 1970.
31. Mary Lee Bundy and Paul Wasserman, op. cit., p. 29. Similar observations are made by Eldred Smith, op. cit., p. 10.
32. For the rules regarding one such operation, see University of Oklahoma Library, "Minutes of the Faculty Meeting, 19 November, 1968" (Norman, Okla.: Mimeo.), Appendix, pp. 1–4.
33. See John J. Corson, *Governance of Colleges and Universities* (New York: McGraw-Hill, 1960), pp. 34–35.

34. Mary Lee Bundy and Paul Wasserman, op. cit., p. 18.
35. Robert Vosper, "Needed: An Open End Career Policy," *A.L.A. Bulletin* 56 (Oct., 1962): 833–835.
36. American Association of University Professors, *Academic Freedom and Tenure: A Handbook of the American Association of University Professors*, ed. by Louis Joughin (Madison: University of Wisconsin Press, 1967), pp. 33–39.
37. "Tenure in Libraries: A Statement of Principles of Intellectual Freedom and Tenure Adopted by the Council of the American Library Association, June 21, 1946," *A.L.A. Bulletin* 40 (Nov., 1946): 451–453.
38. Fay M. Blake, "Tenure for the Academic Librarian," *College and Research Libraries* 29 (Nov., 1968): 504.
39. For a collection of pertinent items, see R. B. Downs, ed., *The First Freedom: Liberty and Justice in the World of Books and Reading* (Chicago: American Library Association, 1960).
40. Lewis C. Branscomb, "Tenure for Professional Librarians at Colleges and Universities," *College and Research Libraries* 26 (July, 1965): 297–298, 341. See also Fay M. Blake, op. cit.
41. See Arthur M. McAnally, "Privileges and Obligations of Faculty Status," *College and Research Libraries* 24 (Mar., 1963): 102–108. Also the survey of practices by Carl Hintz, "Criteria for Appointment to and Promotion in Academic Rank," *College and Research Libraries* 29 (Sept., 1968): 341–346, and especially the proposed policy statement on p. 346.
42. A fine example typical of these is University of Oregon Library, "Final Report, 1968/69 University of Oregon Committee on Promotion and Tenure, to the University Librarian, May 1, 1969" (Eugene, Ore.: The Library, 1969).
43. Anita R. Schiller, op. cit., p. 63 ff.
44. William H. Jesse and Ann E. Mitchell, "Professional Staff Opportunities for Study and Research," *College and Research Libraries* 29 (Mar., 1968): 88.
45. Anita R. Schiller, op. cit., p. 40.
46. Cornell University Libraries, *Report of the Committee on Continuing Education and Professional Growth* (Ithaca, N.Y.: The Libraries, 1969).
47. William H. Jesse and Ann E. Mitchell, op. cit.
48. Some state boards of higher education, in library staffing formulas, have recognized that staffing needs for supporting staff vary percentagewise according to size, and have developed sliding scale formulas. Thus a small library might end up with a 50 : 50 distribution of professional : supporting, whereas larger libraries might be provided a staff of one fourth professional and three fourths supporting. See Arthur M. McAnally, "Budgets by Formula," *Library Quarterly* 33 (Apr., 1963): 159–171.
49. There are numerous articles on this subject. The problem is discussed by a staff in Cornell University Libraries, op. cit., p. 11 ff. See also W. J. Brooking, "Emerging Patterns of Technician Employment with Implications for Libraries," *LED Newsletter* 67 (1968): 11–20.
50. See "The Union Question" (editorial), *Library Journal* 93 (Nov. 1, 1968): 4077, and issues of *C.U. Voice*, the union journal issued at Berkeley since 1965.
51. Eldred Smith, op. cit., p. 11.
52. Wilhelm Munthe, op. cit., pp. 116–117.

53. For evidence of this changing attitude among the faculty, see David O. Lane, "The Selection of Academic Library Materials, a Literature Survey," *College and Research Libraries* 29 (Sept., 1968): 364–372. Also, Eldred Smith, op. cit., p. 9; and Peter Spyers-Duran, ed., *Approval and Gathering Plans in Academic Libraries* (Littleton, Colo.: Published for Western Michigan University by Libraries Unlimited, 1969).

54. William H. Jesse and Ann E. Mitchell, op. cit. See also Robert L. Vosper, "Libraries and the Inquiring Mind," *A.L.A. Bulletin* 59 (Sept., 1965): 709–717. Also for conditions favorable to research and publication, Masse Bloomfield, "The Writing Habits of Librarians," *College and Research Libraries* 27 (March, 1966): 109–119.

55. A sound evaluation of present conditions and reasonable estimate of future trends and needs in research libraries is American Council of Learned Societies, Committee on Research Libraries, *On Research Libraries; Statement and Recommendations, Submitted to the National Advisory Commission on Libraries, November, 1967* (Cambridge, Mass.: M.I.T. Press, c1969).

56. Tefko Sarocevic and Alan M. Rees, "The Impact of the Information Science on Library Practice," *Library Journal* 93 (Nov. 1, 1968): 4097–4101. Mary Lee Bundy and Paul Wasserman (op. cit.) consider this subject at length.

57. Anita R. Schiller, op. cit., p. 27.

58. University of Oklahoma Libraries, *Minutes of the Faculty Meeting of 16 July 1970* (Norman, Okla.: Mimeo), pp. 1–3 and Appendix.

59. See David G. Brown, *The Mobile Professors* (Washington: American Council on Education, 1967). Also, Theodore Caplow and Reece J. McGee, *The Academic Market Place* (New York: Basic Books, 1958), and Howard D. Marshall, *The Mobility of College Faculties* (New York: Pageant Press, 1964).

60. Anita R. Schiller, op. cit., pp. 46–47.

About the Author

Arthur McAnally, Director of Libraries at the University of Oklahoma, is a leading exponent of the Library Faculty. He brought a steadily growing record of good administrative experience to his assignment with Downs at Illinois as Assistant Director for Public Service from 1949 to 1951. It was in that library, with its great leadership in personnel practice, that McAnally found his early models for thinking on this topic. He has since written and worked extensively in this field and has fully developed his own staff in the Library Faculty pattern. He too has taught and traveled to remote areas, notably Peru and Turkey, and is active in professional association work.

INTERLIBRARY COOPERATION

by Robert H. Blackburn

Interlibrary cooperation, like motherhood, is a concept widely respected, an activity carried on by many for the benefit of all, a mystery about which there are still many things to be learned. Nobody will speak against it, but everyone knows that it should not be carried too far. It should not be entered into lightly without due thought being given to continuity, compatibility, legality, and the adequacy of manpower and finance. And for those who embark upon it, no matter how circumspect or "starry-eyed about the business,"[1] it is bound to provide anxieties and some disappointments.

So much has been written about library cooperation, explicit and implicit, fact and fiction, that nobody can read it all or even refer to more than a small part of it. The word cooperation is, of course, used in many different ways and in its broadest sense can include the whole of library science. Any library planned for the use of more than one person is a cooperative resource. The operation of any research library depends upon the meshing of complicated tasks performed by many people applying different skills in various departments. Thus, the building of an academic book collection depends upon the beneficent interaction of library staff, teaching staff, and fiscal authorities; each of these relationships involves a kind of cooperation which is essential but which can more properly be called internal coordination. Interlibrary cooperation, on the other hand, is that which occurs across jurisdictional boundaries, between or among libraries that operate under separate fiscal authorities. It consists of interaction and interdependence, as Stephen McCarthy has said,[2] and it involves a relationship from which each partner is free to withdraw. It is this quality of being voluntary which distinguishes cooperation from other forms of interaction and which creates some of its peculiar difficulties.

The aims of interlibrary cooperation are seldom stated but fairly obvious. From the point of view of the user, his library is a place to obtain the recorded information he wants at any given moment, and if the library cannot serve him adequately with its own holdings, it should be able to call upon or direct him to other sources, regardless of cost. From the point of view of university trustees or state treasurers who pay the cost but who often may have little understanding of the requirements, cooperation spells economy. To them it seems obvious that libraries would cost less if they would only share the work and collections of others, indeed that two or more might live as cheaply as one if they behaved as one. Librarians are in the middle, as usual, feeling responsibility to trustees and to users, both present and future. Their strong sympathy is on the side of the users, and since the potential needs of users are without limit and far wider than the resources of any one library, librarians are naturally attracted to schemes which enable them to reach beyond their own collections toward the whole universe of recorded thought. Their fascination is, however, tempered by awareness that cooperative schemes may sometimes be more costly than other means of achieving the same objectives, or may involve serious practical difficulties, or may create serious inconvenience to local users who are notoriously intolerant of inconveniences which touch themselves. Librarians know that research libraries are unaffected by the parable of loaves and fishes, and cannot feed their multitudes by sharing impoverished collections.[3] They know that libraries cannot hope to operate at a profit and should be closed down if economy were the principal aim. What they must do, in the face of conflicting pressures, is simply to seek the most effective means of using locally available resources for the benefit of present and future readers, and to use interlibrary cooperation as a means of doing certain things which can be done most effectively in that way. The aim is not merely to improve service, or to save money, but rather to assure the maximum use of available resources.

There are, of course, various grades of interaction among libraries. John Cory speaks of four levels or "generations," beginning with casual sharing between independent libraries, proceeding through some banding together of similar libraries, concerted action among different types of libraries, and culminating in networks consisting of various kinds of libraries and nonlibrary agencies with overlapping purposes. Cory uses the term "federalism" to describe the voluntary yielding of some authority, by individual libraries, to some central agency or through a multilateral contract, in order to obtain common benefit.[4] I think federalism may be too strong a word to describe the relationships that have existed or may exist within the community of research libraries, but it does suggest a partial loss of independence implicit in the practical recognition of interdependence.

Cooperation is practiced by research libraries in many ways and for many different purposes, each instance bearing resemblance to others but each shaped by its particular combination of institutions, circumstances, and personalities. These instances are difficult to classify into distinct categories or to discuss in a connected way. Ten years ago Ralph Esterquest published a useful description of twelve types.[5] In another context and with different examples, Robert Downs has defined nine headings,[6] and James Lehman has extended the list to fourteen.[7] Others have sliced the subject in other ways. Any subdividing of the subject can be only indicative and arbitrary, since its varied manifestations may be distinguishable but not separable. For the present purpose, I shall arbitrarily use four general headings. The first has to do with cooperation in providing physical access to the published record as it exists in library collections. The second has to do with bibliographic access, through union catalogs, directories, and other tools by means of which a reader may be made aware of accessible resources beyond the holdings of his own library. The third is cooperation in the building of collections. The fourth, which is directly related to the other three but warrants some separate attention, I have called administration. Under each heading I shall mention some examples, past or present, and venture a guess about future developments.

PHYSICAL ACCESS

A library may make its collections available to readers outside its own area of formal responsibility in two ways. It may receive such readers as visitors, or it may send material to another library for their use. It is hard to imagine any library that would never, under any circumstances, open its collections to outsiders. The tradition of wandering scholars is very old, and the expectation of library hospitality is deeply ingrained in it. The hospitality offered in the research library is subject to restrictions and precautions of varied intensity, designed to protect the collections and the particular rights of users who dwell within the library's formal responsibility.

Institute libraries in German universities, for instance, are generally available only to members of the institute except by special permission of the director.[8] At the Bibliothèque Nationale in Paris, a foreign (or native) university graduate may gain entrance to the reading room by presenting an official letter of introduction and making formal application. At Cambridge, "strangers who desire specially to examine any manuscripts or rare books in the Library may be allowed to do so at the discretion of the Librarian"; a person who is not a member of the Senate and does not hold a university appointment but who wishes regular admission to the library may be granted a card by the Library Syndicate, for a fee, after he has presented an application "together with a letter from two members of the Senate certifying from personal knowledge that the applicant is a student in some specific field, and is a fit and proper person to be admitted to the Library for the said purpose."[9] And in "exceptional cases" the Syndicate may also authorize such a person to borrow books.

In North America, academic libraries in college towns and small cities have usually been comparatively open and liberal in their acceptance of visitors, who are mostly local professional people and students home on vacation. In larger urban centers, the research libraries still try to be liberal to scholars who come from far places to use special collections for a few days or weeks, but many have found it necessary to protect themselves from being swamped by thousands of local outsiders including the staff and students of other educational institutions in the same neighborhood. One may be hospitable to a cricket or two on the hearth, but not to a swarm of locusts; the number of visiting students and research workers can pass the point at which they can be treated casually as guests. At Los Angeles and Toronto, visiting students from other institutions may read freely, while at Harvard and Chicago they may read only for special reasons and by special arrangement; they may not borrow, for outside use, but other visitors who wish to become regular readers or borrowers may make written application and pay a fee. The fee, either by session or by year, is usually stiff enough to screen out casual applicants, and in some universities is comparable to the library fee paid by enrolled students.

Academic libraries in some regions have entered into various degrees of reciprocity in these matters. In 1967 the fourteen provincial universities of Ontario entered into a "cooperative use" agreement which formalizes library visiting privileges, but not borrowing privileges, for staff and graduate students. Twelve of the institutions scattered along the five-hundred-mile route from Ottawa to Windsor operate a daily station wagon service on which library visitors are welcome to travel if they wish. A more recent agreement among Quebec universities provides reciprocity in borrowing as well as visiting by staff and graduate students. By a new agreement between the four state-supported universities in Indiana, each library grants full services to any staff member or student from the other three, and each library pays into a fund (roughly in proportion to benefits received) which pays the salary of a librarian whose special duty is to assist visitors at each of the two larger libraries. In Britain, the University Grants Committee has been advised that university libraries should do as much as they can to serve the members of the other institutions in their own areas, but also that "additional finance should be made available to any university libraries which will have to meet the special needs of students and teachers at neighboring institutions of higher education."[10]

Additional money is certainly needed and will have to be provided sooner or later where additional loads are to be carried, since collections and staff cannot be stretched indefinitely, but money alone is not the whole answer. The recent burgeoning of graduate study and research within established universities, and the growth of new institutions of various kinds, have far outstripped the growth of libraries needed to support them. The resulting pressures from inside and outside the universities, as well as the pressures of growing internal complexity, are forcing large libraries to become more restrictive. Robert Vosper, speaking of the "nearly unbearable level of competition" for UCLA materials, says "thus far we have been able to deal somewhat with this competition only by steadily reducing the generosity of our lending rules even on campus."[11]

As the number of readers increases, this trend can be expected to continue. Sharper distinctions will be made between expendable "teaching" collections and permanent research collections. There will likely be increasing restriction on lending and on access to shelves. Increasingly, service to extramural users may be rendered on the basis of fees or subsidies. These eventualities could be interpreted as a decline in cooperation among libraries, but they may also be thought of as an increase of participation, among all users, in the maintenance of services and preservation of collections for the benefit of all.

The other kind of physical access, provided through interlibrary lending, requires less comment here. Instances of it are reported at least as early as the Ptolemies,[12] and its function is mentioned by nearly everyone who writes about interlibrary cooperation. Its essential ingredients are a known and desired text at one end, an eager reader at the other, willingness in both libraries, and a means of transmitting the text.

The willingness of the lending library is, of course, influenced by the rarity and fragility of the matter requested, the extent of local demand for it, and the nature of local regulations. Problems in these areas may sometimes be solved by sending microfilm or photocopy instead of the original printed piece, and indeed it has become customary for rare material and journal articles to be "lent" in copy rather than in original form.

The willingness of the borrowing library, and the eagerness of the reader, are influenced by the probable cost and promptness of the service. In Britain, good postal service, and a National Lending Library for Science and Technology whose function is specifically to lend by mail, have combined to make mail service a reasonably acceptable substitute for infrequently used books and journal files in the reader's own library. In Sweden, interloan is facilitated at least psychologically by the fact that university libraries pay no postage on their mail.[13] In Europe, generally, research material can be found quickly because it is usually on shelves to which readers have no direct access, and many scholars in their own local libraries are accustomed to applying for local material and waiting for it to be brought later, not necessarily on the same day. The difference between obtaining local material and obtaining material through interloan may, therefore, be comparatively small and tolerable. There is a significant flow of interloans even across national borders; it is reported that Soviet libraries lend more than 12,000 volumes a year to more than forty countries.[14]

In North America, on the other hand, postal service is slower, and readers are accustomed to getting most of their books by hand directly from the shelf. Interloan may, therefore, seem to be intolerably slow by comparison and in fact it is sometimes weeks from the time a reader makes a request before he has the book in hand. Some time can of course be saved if there is a means of quick location, such as the teletype service based on the union catalogue in the National Library of Canada, and if loans are requested by teletype. A daily delivery service such as the one operated by the universities in Ontario,[15] and the similar Quebec service, which now connects with the Ontario route at the University of Ottawa, can also save time and offer other advantages. For instance, a van service may provide gentler handling of the material. It may reduce one restraint by obscuring the transit cost of individual packages ("it costs nothing, because the van goes every day anyway") and as traffic grows it can in fact become cheaper than mailing. Transmission of photocopy by telefacsimile, rather than by post or courier, takes only about five minutes per page but is still too expensive to be practical for general use. The time to be saved on the actual transit of requests and material is probably less important, however, than the time which might be saved by more expeditious handling of requests within both the borrowing and lending libraries. To be sure there is much verifying, locating, preparing, notifying, and acknowledging to be done, but unless it is deliberately given a high priority, an interloan transaction naturally tends to be put aside in favor of those that involve readers standing at the counter and material that is at hand.

It is obvious that a research worker needs access to a library where most of the material he needs will be at hand.[16] For practical reasons he must discount the value of material in remote libraries, which he can use only by interloan, and for various reasons he may set the rate of discount very high. Reference librarians seem to have the impression that one quarter to one half of the professors and graduate students who ask for help after failing to find what they want, decide to abandon the search when the desired material proves to be unavailable locally. In North America at least, most readers seem to apply a heavy discount on remote collections, a higher rate than that applied by librarians who think mainly in terms of the time required to locate items, and different again from the very small discount allowed by fiscal authorities who think in terms of quick and unlimited mobility merging into the magic of telefacsimile.

These rates of discount are, of course, all highly subjective, and the discrepancies can lead to serious misunderstandings and mistakes. As Edwin Williams says, "individual universities . . . may be tempted to rely on co-operation excessively and embark on programmes for which their own resources are seriously insufficient."[17] On the other hand, individual scholars may ignore remote resources, which are in fact reasonably available.

These discrepancies and dangers of wishful thinking might perhaps be diminished by objective analysis, such as one finds in Gordon Williams' study of the comparative costs of borrowing and owning journals.[18] Cost studies are needed, especially, and may help to establish the funding and staffing needed to put the service on a realistic basis.

Meanwhile, the New York State University Interlibrary Loan program (NYSILL) is an interesting development[19] in a direction charted some years ago by the Ministry of Education in West-Rhine-Westphalia.[20] In the NYSILL program, libraries that have accepted designation as resource collections in particular subjects receive a basic annual subsidy, plus $2.50 per request searched, plus $2.00 per request filled. In an experimental extension of this program Cornell University has contracted to give bibliographic and reference service to a fourteen-county region, and receives reimbursement for the salary of a reference librarian plus a payment per transaction. These schemes acknowledge that there is no service which cannot be supported effectively on a business-like scale if the cost is simply a charge on the good will and the spare resources of institutions which are already hard-pressed to meet their own local responsibilities. As the rising tides of publication and research make it more and more necessary for libraries to help each other, we shall probably see a variety of contract arrangements, treaties, fees and subsidies, and cost studies to justify them.

In these paragraphs on transmission of printed text from one library to a reader at another, I have purposely omitted any mention of the possibilities of printing out text from digital storage or microstorage in a remote computer, possibilities about which much is being said and written these days.[21] It seems that if and when either of these possibilities comes about on a practical working scale, it will not really be a new form of publication, attended by its own share of technical, legal, and financial problems. As a form of publication, it will be bought by libraries and used alongside their cuneiform tablets, books, and numerous other surviving forms of recorded thought.

BIBLIOGRAPHIC ACCESS

Before there can be any useful mobility of material among libraries, there has to be a way of knowing what is where. The published catalogs of individual libraries are of very limited value in this respect, especially older ones which tend to cover collections not obtainable on loan. Even the rash of recent ones printed by offset, and covering collections which may be borrowed, are expensive to buy, automatically out of date, and are a slow means of tracking down elusive titles in distant libraries.

Catalogs and lists that cover the holdings of many libraries at once are, of course, more useful from this point of view, and there have been many applications of this idea. They may include general holdings or specific types of holdings such as manuscripts, newspapers, journals, and so on. The Royal Library in Stockholm has published an annual union catalog of foreign literature in Swedish research libraries since 1887.[22] The lamented Gesamtkatalog of the Prussian State Library and ten Prussian universities was nearly completed by 1918.[23] The state libraries in Leningrad and Moscow began a number of specialized union catalogs in the early 1930s.[24] The well-known National Union Catalog compiled by the Library of Congress and published since 1956, the union catalog maintained by the National Central Library in Britain, and the national union catalogs that have been developing in Italy and Canada in the past twenty years are all ambitious attempts to provide bibliographic control over the holdings of important libraries within a whole country.

Involvement of a national library in compiling a union catalog, and in other activities which imply significant interaction among libraries in its country, is really a part of its responsibility and does not fall within a strict definition of cooperation.[25] If the national library has authority over the others, then its actions amount to administrative integration. If it does not, then its own actions as a sponsor or supporter of cooperation may be simply a performance of reasonable duties, the provision of services "paid for by the taxpayer and justified in terms of the national interest."[26] Despite technicalities of definition, however, the objective is to obtain common benefit through collective action; this can hardly be achieved unless the work is undertaken in a cooperative spirit.

Most union catalogs, of course, are not national in scope. In the United States many regional catalogs were founded in the 1930s with labor subsidized by the federal government, most notably those at Seattle, Denver, and Philadelphia. In 1942, Robert Downs edited a description of nearly a hundred union catalogs in the United States[27]; he also chaired a Joint Committee which recommended means of expanding the National Union Catalog.[28] In Britain, the National Central Library compiled its central catalog in the 1930s from ten regional catalogs planned to serve as screens within their own regions.[29] In West Germany after 1945, regional catalogs such as the one at Cologne were formed to facilitate the use of surviving collections of new acquisitions.

Besides the national and regional union catalogs there are, of course, local ones, some formal and some unknown even to the directors of the libraries concerned. Wherever there are two or more neighboring libraries with overlapping interests, their reference librarians are likely to make joint lists of journals or other material of high priority. The same material is likely to be listed also in the more comprehensive union catalogs, but the local list can save time by providing a more comprehensive guide to local locations. The mimeographed *Union List of Selected Medical Periodicals Currently Received in Metropolitan Toronto Medical Libraries,* for example, covers many collections not reported in the latest edition of the printed *Joint Catalogue of Serials in the Libraries of the City of Toronto,* or in the latest edition of *Scientific Serials in Canadian Libraries,* or in the monumental *Union List of Serials in Libraries of the United States and Canada.* From the standpoint of the reader and the librarian assisting him, a closer location spells quicker access, and a local list is the first one to check. National and international lists have far more titles, but fewer local addresses.

It is of course very expensive for a research library to report its holdings, or a selected part of them, to a number of union catalogs, the more so if successive editions require repeated checking by hand. It is also a costly business to compile and edit the reports and to make them available through publication or a referral service, or both. Local and regional lists, if they cover the same ground as national catalogs, may improve promptness but not coverage, and the value of that promptness should always be looked at critically in relation to the cost of gaining it. Many projects have broken down on account of the costs, and others have been discontinued in the expectation that their function may be performed in other ways. The *Joint Catalogue of Serials in the Libraries of the City of Toronto*, for example, was discontinued after the fifth edition, on account of costs, and has been superseded by the computer-compiled serial catalogs of the National Library and National Science Library in Ottawa. It would, in fact, be possible to have a Toronto catalog printed out separately by the national libraries. While such a listing would not cover all the collections that are covered by the old *Joint Catalogue*, it would be better in every way to make the national list more inclusive than to begin again on a new and separate list. Robert Downs, weighing the virtues of local versus national lists, has said "after having been a student of union catalog problems for more than 20 years, I am convinced that maximum development of the National Union Catalog should be the prime objective of any union catalog program for the country."[30]

As long as the shared use of many libraries continues to be the only means of meeting the needs of scholars, the need for union catalogs seems almost inescapable. The burden of maintaining them, if it is allowed to decrease their coverage and quality, will defeat the purpose, since better and quicker service is needed. Our best hope seems to be that national union catalogs can be mechanized, be expanded selectively to include reporting important within regions and metropolitan areas, and be kept up to date and quickly available. This is a tall order indeed, and there are many important problems to be solved concerning scope, organization, finance, and technology, but much hopeful exploration is taking place. One example is the SUNY Biomedical Communication Network, which began operation in 1968 with headquarters at the University of Syracuse. This is an interesting experiment employing a computer linked to consoles in the participating libraries.[31]

In exploring these new possibilities, it is to be hoped that questions of *what* will not be settled by default or by the expediencies of *how*. There must be a decision, for instance, as to whether a union catalog should be more than a simple tool for locating copies of works by particular authors. Should it provide additional bibliographic detail and subject analysis which can be used as a standard and source for cataloging in other libraries? Should it try to provide a subject approach for users who are pursuing a subject rather than an author? What other approaches should it provide, if any? What relationship should it bear to the national bibliography of its own country, and of other countries? How inclusive should it be as to language, date, form of material, and libraries reported? Ideal answers to such questions should be propounded, and tentative priorities set, before technical and financial realities are given too much weight.

As a supplement to author-oriented union catalogs, or as a very imperfect substitute, there are many published surveys of resources. One of the most ambitious of these is the four-volume *Special Library Resources* published by the Special Libraries Association. It is now more than twenty years out of date but even when new, it was a rather uneven help in guessing where particular material might be. Guides to subject collections continue to appear,[32] however, and are apparently useful enough to justify the work put into them by libraries and editors. Other surveys, such as those conducted in Canada by Edwin Williams in 1962 and Robert Downs in 1967, contain brief descriptions and assessments of subject collections, but their real impact is administrative and political rather than bibliographic.

A more useful but less used substitute for the union catalog is the comprehensive "backstop" collection. Thus, a British librarian knows, without pausing to look it up anywhere, that any scientific or technical book or journal, within defined limits, is available at the National Lending Library for Science and Technology. In America, any European doctoral dissertation or any scientific journal, within defined limits, is available at the Center for Research Libraries. This principle, if carried far enough, could obviate the need for union catalogs of any kind, but meanwhile it leads to my third heading.

ACQUISITION

Before reciprocal physical access and bibliographic access among libraries can be of use, there must of course be collections worth sharing. The pooling of inadequate collections can only produce what Robert

Vosper has called a "pool of frustrated readers." As Verner Clapp puts it, in distinguishing library "networks" from other kinds, "it is the content rather than channel that makes the network"[33] as far as libraries are concerned.

The great majority of cooperative library schemes, which concentrate on the channels, the means of providing bibliographic and physical access, assume that the libraries involved, each building its own collection for its own purposes, will somehow manage among them to assemble all the material that is needed. This assumption is not entirely valid, since no library can acquire more than a small fraction of world publication and it does not necessarily choose material that other libraries have passed over; indeed, the ordinary tools and practices applied to book selection tend to make choices coincident rather than complementary.

If the collections of various libraries are to complement each other, it is obvious that a plan is needed. It is not so obvious how a plan can be made or carried out. Local ad hoc agreements are fairly common—a public reference library and a neighboring college library may agree to divide responsibility for maintaining files of the *New York Times* and the London *Times*—but cannot really make a difference to the general problem. Robert Downs has cited examples of local working agreements going back to the nineteenth century.[34] Union catalogs are sometimes proposed as tools which could be used in planning or carrying out agreements on specialization among libraries, but "there is no evidence to show that any important use has been made of these tools for these purposes."[35] For planning, which must deal in broad categories rather than individual items, they are of less use than general surveys and directories, though these latter also have their limitations.

Again the aims rather than techniques should govern, lest the effort should disintegrate into an attempt to slice up libraries by subject field. The principal aim is to provide each library with reasonable access to a "backstop" of material which it may need from time to time but cannot afford to have in its own collection. A secondary but still very important aim is to save money by reducing the need of individual libraries to acquire marginal material as insurance against future needs. The extent to which either of these aims can be realized is conditional on the accessibility and dependability of the backstop.

Schemes for providing the backstop may be organized by subject or source of the material, or by a combination of the two. The most usual approach is to assign subject specialties among the participating libraries, but it is full of difficulties. Classification schemes are notoriously arbitrary, notoriously subject to varied interpretation, and not applicable until after the material has arrived in participating libraries. The significant literature of a subject may include forms, sources, and languages with which the assigned library may be quite unable to cope; much of the relevant material may, therefore, be missed or ignored by the assigned library, or if acquired, may sit uncataloged and unavailable. On the other hand, variations of interpretation may lead to much overlapping with the purchases of other libraries which have accepted responsibility for related subjects. Moreover, since few subjects are served by comprehensive up-to-date bibliographies, it is difficult to sample or check on the performance of the system to be sure that assignments are in fact being carried out without serious gaps or redundancy.

Some of these problems are avoided if a scheme is based on each participant undertaking to acquire all the significant publications of a country or countries. This kind of scheme is more efficient as far as acquisition and cataloging are concerned, and if followed consistently could obviate the need for union catalogs. It has been attractive to libraries that support "area studies" but less attractive to others where it is supposed that the assigned category should be simply an extension of a good existing subject collection. The logic of this supposition applies only within the single library, not within the remainder of the system, and there is some doubt as to whether an effective backstop system can really consist of a complex of local subject collections closely related to the daily work of local users.

Notable examples of jointly planned acquisition programs are recent and few, and so well known that they do not require lengthy description here. The Farmington Plan established by the Association of Research Libraries in 1948, to bring into the United States one copy of every important foreign book, is based on the voluntary acceptance of responsibility by member libraries. It began with the idea that current books would be acquired centrally and assigned to members, but soon became a decentralized operation in which individual libraries administer subject assignments (for material from Western Europe) and assignments by country for other parts of the world. The West German Sondersammelgebiet plan established in 1949 was different in that assignment of subjects was based on a carefully selected classified list of about 6,000 foreign journals, and participation was encouraged and facilitated in the first few years by significant grants of money from the Forschungsgemeinschaft.[36] The Specialization Scheme begun in England in 1950 by the Southeastern Regional Library System,[37] designed for the comprehensive purchase of English books by public libraries, solved problems of classification by having each participant buy every book listed in a particular subject of the *British National Bibliography*. The ABC Plan adopted by Swedish county libraries in 1955 applies to foreign literature, each county being responsible for the "subject group denoted in the Swedish classification system by the same letter found on the license plates of cars registered in that county."[38] The Scandia Plan, which grew up in 1959 out of an early agreement among the four Swedish universities, is different in that it includes the principal libraries of four countries, it involves an obligation to acquire both old and new material in a subject, and it is concerned mostly with subjects which are "of limited and markedly peripheral interest"[39] in Scandinavia.

It is typical of these schemes that they do not restrict the freedom of action of any of the participants, apart from the assigned task. This condition is necessary if participation of independent institutions is to be enlisted, but it is also a severe limitation upon what can be accomplished. Anything beyond a very minor commitment of time and money to the system, on the part of any member, must interfere with that member's ability to meet local needs, and cannot be seriously contemplated unless the system provides for at least partial remuneration of costs.

It must be remembered that university libraries, which comprise the majority of research collections in each country, are not constituted so that they may enter freely into joint agreements on specialization, or other cooperative projects, no matter how logical or widely beneficial such projects may be. At least in the English-speaking countries they are linked closely to the academic programs of their universities, and are answerable to their presidents or to academic committees for the way they support such programs. A librarian cannot make an independent decision to ignore some part of the academic program, or to commit significant funds to activities that do not bear an obvious relationship to the program. Really major subject specialization among university libraries can occur only if it is parallel with specialization among the universities themselves, in their long-range programs of teaching and research. In some jurisdictions, such as California, delimitation and co-ordination of the academic programs in state institutions are decided centrally at the state level; in others such as Ontario, valiant efforts are being made by the universities themselves to integrate their programs by voluntary agreement.[40] Either way, and in spite of much urging to the contrary, the joint planning of really effective collection-building plans within a state's research libraries can begin only after the pattern of academic programs is firmly established.

The Scandia plan is international, and the others mentioned above range from national to regional. This variety raises a question about the best size of unit for such a venture. A state or province may seem a con-venient unit because the distances are manageable, the people know each other, and institutions operate at least under the same laws if not under the same funding agency. A whole country offers advantages as a unit, since a national plan may be assisted by the national library and the national budget. The whole world would offer the ideal unit as far as breadth and depth of coverage are concerned, but the worst for ease of bibliographic and physical access. The best size unit is surely the one that yields the best possible compromise between breadth and promptness of access to research material. Breadth is improved by adding more and more large or specialized libraries to the scheme. Promptness is improved by having good channels to the material and as few chan-nels as possible—a single channel would be the ideal. D. J. Urquhart, speaking from a rather special point of view about the English regional schemes that attempt to be self-sufficient in English publications, makes strong cases for a centralized national lending collection which could serve as a backstop in its own country and have connections with similar collections in other countries.[41] Writing from a similar point of view, Ralph Esterquest wrote that "the decentralization principle, based upon subject specialization, is mostly a false hope" and that "what progress has been made toward controlling co-operatively the ever-increasing flow of materials has usually been made through centralized pools."[42]

The outstanding example of a centralized pool of jointly owned re-search material is, of course, the Center for Research Libraries in Chi-cago. It began in 1950 as a joint storage center of seldom-used material deposited by a number of large university libraries in the Midwest (including, naturally, the University of Illinois). It began also with a small and rather cautious program of joint purchases. The acquisition program, supported by membership fees and assisted by the National Science Foundation (1955 onward) and the Higher Education Act of 1966, has helped to create a loan collection of significance far beyond the Midwest. Its membership now extends from coast to coast and into Canada, among libraries which have adopted the view that having access to seldom-used material which is jointly owned, although remote, is an economical and acceptable alternative to owning the material fully and locally. There is now federal legislation which could help the center to become a comprehensive national lending library of foreign publications, and such a development might be in keeping with the center's evolution to date. The cost of maintaining a national collection, meanwhile, bears heavily on the few dozen members, and membership rules were revised recently to spread the cost more equitably among all regular users. Though the center has an occasional visitor, it has no local population of readers to serve; it is a dedicated lending service to other libraries. While it has published its catalog, most of its holdings are in broad categories (theses, state documents, scientific journals), which can be housed and used without having to be cataloged.

Another library dedicated entirely to lending by mail is the British National Lending Library for Science and Technology at Boston Spa. It is different from the center in that it deals mainly with current publications in a more limited field, and it is state supported. It has, however, dramatized the advantages of a centralized backstop collection and, like the center, it is evolving in scope and experimenting with service beyond the borders of its own country. Along with the center, it is an example to be pondered by those who wish to establish backstop collections.

ADMINISTRATION

Under this heading I shall mention briefly some of the cooperative activities that facilitate joint acquisitions and collective access, both bibliographic and physical, but that do not fit comfortably under any of those rubrics.

Cooperative storage of seldom-used material, for instance, is a concept strongly advocated by some librarians and many university presidents. Presidents were among the strong proponents of the Midwest Interlibrary Center, the prime example of joint storage. The center was indeed economical storage, since the site and the building were donated and much of the material deposited in it, never having been cataloged in its home libraries, did not involve alteration of records. Other storage projects would have to match these conditions to be as good a bargain, and now that the center itself is full it has to rent space, since it has no money for additional construction. The center has also reduced the total bulk of deposits by discarding duplicates, but this sort of compacting could be accomplished by a group of libraries for their cataloged material, without centralizing the residue. Several universities, having considered the costs of remoteness and of altering records (including national union catalogs), have decided in favor of cheap local storage. Those which decide otherwise, in favor of pooled storage, should weigh the relative advantages of regional and national pools.

Cooperative approaches to the very serious problem of deteriorating paper have not yet had the attention or support they deserve. The deterioration of wood-pulp paper is far advanced in much library material published in the present century, and some is already beyond use. Even research material that is protected from the ravages of relative classification systems, central heating, polluted air, and photocopiers is not out of danger, since chemical deterioration is inherent in the paper and bindings. Studies of the durability of paper and methods of de-acidification, conducted under the auspices of the Association of Research Libraries since 1960 and supported by the Council on Library Resources, have made an impression on some paper makers and some university presses, but much remains to be done to improve the durability of future publications. An even greater and more urgent effort is needed if existing collections are to be rescued. The research library community is faced with an acquisition problem in reverse: how can at least one copy of every existing work be preserved and made available to future scholars? In a paper written for the Association of Research Libraries, Gordon Williams has proposed the best answer so far—a national "library of record" which would receive the best available copies of deteriorating books, de-acidify them, keep them in cold storage, and microfilm them on demand in order to supply copies.[43] It proposes cold storage rather than immediate filming for reasons of economy, for the sake of preserving the original as long as possible, because of present uncertainty about the durability of microfilm, and because the potential of high-ratio miniaturization has not been fully explored. This proposal, or alternatives to it,[44] will obviously require cooperation on a large scale by research libraries and by funding agencies, if effective action is to be taken in time.

Microfilming of rare or fragile material has often been done jointly to preserve the text or to provide library copies. The Canadian newspaper microfilm project of the Canadian Librarian Association has run for twenty years on the principle that the cost of making a negative can be split among three libraries which buy positive copies. The foreign newspaper project of the Association of Research Libraries, administered by the Center for Research Libraries, takes the next logical step by assuming that one loanable positive is cheaper than three and ordinarily can meet the collective demands made upon it. The large commercial sets of microfilm do serve to preserve text (or at least the better ones do). But, unfortunately, they skim off the cream of material in current demand from which a comprehensive joint project, sponsored by the libraries themselves, might derive some income to help it deal with the remaining ninety-nine percent—which is skim milk, nourishing and necessary, but less glamorous.

Cooperative processing is a term that covers a broad range of aspirations and some activities. It may be used to describe such operations as the three-year project in which the University of Toronto, under contract, selected, bought, and produced book catalogs for identical basic collections for five new colleges which needed basic libraries in a hurry. It certainly describes the centralized operation recently begun in Colorado and being planned in Ohio. One aspect of it is involved in another sort of ABC plan adopted in 1969 by the three British Columbia universities, in which each library gives rushed cataloging to titles, beginning with specified letters of the alphabet.

It appears that under careful control, a fairly wide range of technical processes may be performed centrally for several smallish institutions of similar scope. Centralization may effect some economies if multiple copies can be bought and cataloged simultaneously for several collections, so long as there is no need to integrate this material into older local collections. The nature and complexity of large research collections are quite a different matter, and such institutions can hardly consider centralized processing except in such a context as the Joint University Libraries—a separate corporation that provides a consolidated library service to three universities in Nashville.

Research libraries have a great deal to gain, both in economy and speed of cataloging, from the sharing of catalog copy. Most shared copy is, of course, that which is distributed at cost by national libraries. This has been done by the Library of Congress since 1901, by the National Diet Library of Japan since 1950 and, more recently, by the National Library of Canada. The amount of copy available has been increased significantly over the past three years by the national plan for acquisition and cataloging, carried out by the Library of Congress under legislation initiated by the Association of Research Libraries. The agreements made by the Library of Congress with national libraries in other countries, to facilitate prompt cataloging of an increased flow of acquisitions, constitute an exciting and significant development in international cooperation.

The sharing of catalog copy, whether for local consumption or union catalogs, requires agreement on certain standards of bibliographic format. Such standards have been the substance of continuing debate, national and international, and recent initiatives of the International Federation of Library Associations have produced a very favorable climate for standardization.

To facilitate the sharing of catalog copy and other bibliographic information by computers, the Library of Congress has produced the MARC II format as a medium of communication. In planning, testing, and revising the format, the Library of Congress worked closely with a number of selected libraries of various kinds. Consultation and cooperation continue on a broad base as England and France and other countries work out their own extensions of the MARC format. The result, once it becomes really operational, will establish a new kind of interdependence among libraries.

There is much more that could be said. Like motherhood, library cooperation is an endless subject, and each instance produces its own joys and sorrows. Unlike motherhood, it is set in a tradition in which vague and casual relationships have been the norm, but a tradition which is being moved by various forces towards more specific agreements and formal structures. I have tried to indicate some of the forces and directions as I see them.

References

1. Robert B. Downs, "Library Co-operation and Specialization," in *Problems and Prospects of the Research Library*, ed. by Edwin E. Williams for Association of Research Libraries (New Brunswick: Scarecrow Press, 1955), p. 93.
2. Stephen A. McCarthy, "Library Interaction and Interdependence," *Library Lectures* 18 (Mar. 28, 1966): 23–36.
3. Douglas Bryant, "Memorandum on the Library of Congress," *Congressional Record* CVIII:83 (May 24, 1962): 8481–8483.
4. John M. Cory, "Library Federalism," *Proceedings of the 67th Annual Conference, Ontario Library Association* 31 (Jan., 1961): 71–89.
5. Ralph T. Esterquest, "Co-operation in Library Services," *Library Quarterly* 31 (Jan., 1961): 71–89.
6. Robert B. Downs, *Resources of Canadian Academic and Research Libraries* (Ottawa: Association of Universities and Colleges of Canada, 1967), pp. 163–183.
7. James O. Lehman, "Co-operation Among Small Academic Libraries," *College and Research Libraries* 30:6 (Nov., 1969): 491–497.
8. J. Periam Danton, *Book Selection and Collections: A Comparison of German and American University Libraries* (New York: Columbia University Press, 1963), p. 49.
9. *Statutes and Ordnances of the University of Cambridge* (Cambridge: University Press, 1967), p. 447.
10. University Grants Committee, *Report of the Committee on Libraries* (London: HMSO, 1967), p. 158.
11. *Report of the University Librarian, 1966/67* (Los Angeles: University of California), p. 8.
12. "The Letter of Aristeas," in *The Apocrypha and Pseudepigrapha of the Old Testament in English*, ed. by R. H. Charles, v. 2 (Oxford: Clarendon Press, 1963), p. 100, verse 46.
13. Gosta Ottervik, "Swedish Library Cooperation," *Library Journal* 88:20 (Nov. 15, 1963): 4317.
14. M. Rudomino, "International Relations of Soviet Libraries," *Libri* 16 (1966): 62.
15. Ontario Council of University Librarians, *Anniversary Report of the Inter-University Transit System* (Toronto: Committee of Presidents of Ontario Universities, 1968).
16. University Grants Committee, op. cit., p. 50.
17. Edwin E. Williams, *Resources of Canadian University Libraries* (Ottawa: National Conference of Canadian Universities and Colleges, 1962), p. 51.
18. Gordon R. Williams et al., "Library Cost Models: Owning Versus Borrowing Serial Publications," Publication PB182304 for the Office of Scientific Information, National Science Foundation (Bethesda: Westat Research Inc., 1968), p. 161.

19. E. J. Josey, "The Role of the College Library in the 3R's Systems," *Bookmark* (Oct. 1968): 10.
20. Rudolf Juchhoff, "The Present State of Co-operation in Germany," *Library Association Record* 21 (Nov., 1954): 426.
21. J. C. R. Licklider, *Libraries of the Future* (Cambridge: M.I.T. Press, 1965).
22. Ottervik, op. cit., p. 4316.
23. Juchhoff, op. cit., p. 423.
24. J. H. P. Pafford, *Library Co-operation in Europe* (London: Library Association, 1935), p. 200.
25. Curt D. Wormann, "Co-operation of National Libraries with Other Libraries in the Same Country and in Other Countries," *UNESCO Bulletin for Libraries* 18 (1964): 166.
26. Esterquest, op. cit., p. 72.
27. Robert B. Downs, ed., *Union Catalogs in the United States* (Chicago: ALA, 1942), p. 409.
28. Robert B. Downs, "Expanding the National Union Catalog," *ALA Bulletin* 37:11 (Nov. 1943): 434.
29. Robert F. Vollans, *Library Co-operation in Great Britain* (London: National Central Library, 1952), p. 65.
30. Robert B. Downs, Bulletin 11 (1954), Bibliographical Center for Research, Denver. See also "Summary of Regional Libraries Today: A Symposium," *College and Research Libraries* 8:1 (Jan. 1947): 69.
31. Irwin H. Pizer, "Regional Medical Library Network," *Bulletin of the Medical Library Association* 57:2 (Apr., 1969): 101–115.
32. R. C. Lewanski, *Subject Collections in European Libraries: A Directory and Bibliographical Guide* (New York: R. R. Bowker Co., 1965); Lee Ash, *Subject Collections, A Guide to Special Book Collections and Subject Emphases as Reported by University, College, Public and Special Libraries in the United States and Canada,* 3d ed. (New York: R. R. Bowker Co., 1967); Janet Fyfe and R. H. Deutsch, *Directory of Special Collections in Canadian Libraries,* Occasional Paper no. 58 (Ottawa: Canadian Library Association, 1968).
33. Verner W. Clapp, "Public Libraries and the Network Idea," *Literary Journal* 95:2 (Jan., 1970): 123.
34. Robert B. Downs, "American Library Co-operation in Review," *College and Research Libraries* 6:4 (Sept. 1945): 412; Robert B. Downs and Harvie Branscomb, "A Venture into Library Co-operation," *Library Journal* 60:20 (Nov. 15, 1935): 877–879.
35. Esterquest, op. cit., p. 74.
36. Gisele von Busse, "Co-operative Acquisition," *Library Journal* 78:2 (Jan. 15, 1953); Juchhoff, op. cit.
37. Ralph T. Esterquest, *Library Cooperation in the British Isles.* ACRL Monograph no. 12 (Chicago: ACRL, 1955), p. 16.
38. Tonnes Kleberg, "An Outline of the Scandia Plan," *Library Journal* 88:20 (Nov. 15, 1963): 4319.
39. *Ibid.,* p. 4321.
40. *Collective Autonomy, Second Annual Review 1967/68* (Toronto: Committee of Presidents of Universities of Ontario, 1968).

41. D. J. Urquhart, "Co-operation—Local, Regional or National," *Library Association Record* 71:7 (July, 1969): 197–201.
42. Ralph Esterquest, "Co-operation in Library Services," *Library Quarterly* 31:1 (Jan. 1961): 84.
43. Gordon R. Williams, "The Preservation of Deteriorating Books," *Library Journal* 91:1–2 (Jan. 1966): 51054, 189–194.
44. Verner W. Clapp, *The Future of the Research Library* (Urbana: University of Illinois Press, 1964), p. 27 ff.

About the Author

Robert H. Blackburn, in his present function as Chief Librarian of the University of Toronto, presides over the library of the largest academic institution of Canada. He was deeply involved with Bob Downs in the planning for the epochal survey of Canadian academic libraries, led by Downs in 1967. This cooperative effort, and the coordinated character of his own library organization make him logically qualify for the topic of interlibrary cooperation. Blackburn's natural gifts for large administration mark him as Canada's parallel for the Downs of our library world.

LIBRARY RESOURCES AND BIBLIOGRAPHY

by William V. Jackson

In 1938, the American Library Association published *Resources of Southern Libraries,* the first attempt "to study all classes of library research materials over a large region"[1] and the first important contribution of Robert Bingham Downs to the field of library resources. In the thirty-two years that have passed since then, Downs' activities in this area have been so many and so varied that scholars, students, and librarians remain permanently indebted to him. These endeavors have included major publications (e.g., *Resources of New York City Libraries*); numerous articles; surveys and reports dealing in whole or in part with resources (e.g., those for Cornell University, the Richmond area, Kansas City, Brigham Young University); and the compilations which he recently edited on resources of all types of libraries in the states of Missouri and North Carolina. As an outgrowth of his first fifteen years of work, Downs compiled the major key to publications in the field, *American Library Resources, A Bibliographical Guide* (1951), and ten years later a supplement for 1950–1961 (a second supplement covering 1961–70 is in preparation); for the *Library Trends* issue on Research in Librarianship he reviewed the status of and need for research in the resources area.[2] In addition, Downs has twice served as chairman of the (then) Board on Resources of American Libraries, 1939–1942 and 1945–1950, has advised the Library of Congress on the National Union Catalog, and has been chairman of the Association of Research Libraries' Farmington Plan Committee. Not the least of these activities was the introduction, in 1943, of a course entitled "Resources of American Libraries" (Library

Science 427) into the curriculum of the University of Illinois Graduate School of Library Science. He taught this course for a number of years, offering students in both the M.S. and doctoral programs an opportunity to profit from his wide range of experience.

This area represents such an important side of the career of Robert Bingham Downs, that it should be considered in this volume, but the field of library resources has many ramifications and relates to many other aspects of librarianship—for example, collection development and bibliographic control, financing of major libraries, union catalogs and union lists, many types of library cooperation and interinstitutional planning, and spatial needs of libraries. It would not be possible to prepare a complete survey and evaluation of the progress that has taken place in the years spanning Downs' professional career. One important limitation in the very term "library resources," as generally used, is that it relates chiefly to the holdings of university and other research libraries, or collections of a similar nature when they exist in college, state, public, or special libraries. This paper, therefore, considers but one aspect of the field: the published guide to library resources—probably the most important result of activity in the area.

Although one encounters some difficulty in attempting to define "guide to resources" with precision, it is important to remember that such a work is essentially the description—*not* the listing—of special collections and subject strengths in one or more libraries. The descriptive narrative should cover such facts as the nature and extent of holdings, their language and geographic spread, the degree of comprehensiveness, the unique materials (e.g., first editions and manuscripts) and nonbook holdings present, the special emphases or areas of note within the total field being reviewed, and the supporting and related materials in other parts of the collection. The guide does not deal in specific titles, except as examples or as rarities of such significance and/or value that they must be mentioned, nor does it necessarily judge the adequacy of holdings for research purposes. It does not usually compare holdings of one institution with those of another. One might say that the guide should enable its reader to see the range and scope of a special collection or area of subject strength and to visualize its component parts as if they were on shelves before him. E. E. Williams differentiates between the *guide* to resources, whose purpose is the dissemination of information to make collections useful, and the *survey* of resources, whose purpose is to improve the holdings of a particular library or group of libraries. However, as he suggests, it is not wise to push this contrast too far.[3] In fact, much of the published literature uses the two terms without distinction.

One may also discriminate between the guide to resources (as defined above) and works that provide information about resources in other ways. Although Downs included many such "handbooks, check lists, bibliographies, calendars, surveys, union lists, union catalogs and similar guides"[4] in *American Library Resources, A Bibliographical Guide*, their primary purpose is not to describe holdings of either a single institution or a group of libraries, but to provide either brief information (frequently as part of another purpose, such as the handbook or directory giving library hours and services) or the facts as to whether specific items—monographic, serial, or nonbook—are available (such as the list or catalog of holdings). L. R. Wilson some years ago neatly summarized the relationship between the guide and one of these types, the union list, when he expressed their complementary nature: "Whereas union catalogs list and locate specific titles and editions, the surveys of resources indicate areas in which libraries are strong."[5]

It is worth mentioning that to these publications (which are enumerative rather than descriptive in nature) modern technology has contributed two: the printed book catalog, which is enjoying a renaissance as a result of the application of the techniques of photographic reproduction to entire library files by such firms as G. K. Hall; and the printout of serial holdings of individual institutions or cooperating groups of libraries, which is appearing as a consequence of the use of computers for storing data about serial subscriptions and holdings. In fact, it is obvious (without seeking exact statistics) that of the nearly 9,000 publications listed in *American Library Resources* and its supplement (as well as of the additional titles published in the past decade) relatively few are true guides to resources. All, of course, do provide information on resources, but the majority utilize an enumerative rather than a descriptive technique.

Although some publications dealing with resources appeared late in the 19th century, the true guide seems to have flourished in the 1930s and 1940s when the ALA Board (now Committee) on Resources of American Libraries did much to encourage their compilation, in the hope that the movement would eventually lead to a series of guides to all major research collections in the country. Unfortunately, this did not occur, and indeed little seems to have taken place from the late forties through the fifties.

More recently, the availability of federal funds has apparently stimulated a modest flurry of activity, chiefly at the state level, and several publications (as noted below) have appeared since 1965. They generally cover school, smaller public, and special libraries as well as institutions with collections of importance for advanced study and research. Despite such exceptions it remains accurate to say that relatively few new guides (in the sense used in this paper) have come from the presses in recent years. Nevertheless, the total number of titles dealing with resources has increased greatly, as indicated by the fact that the supplement to Downs' bibliography includes, for a ten-year period, about half as many publications as appeared in the basic volume—in other words, an average annual rate of production for the decade about twice that of the average for each year, 1900–1951, covered in the basic volume.

An examination of guides to resources suggests at least eight different types. We can differentiate four by geographic limitations: they are national, regional, state, or local in scope. There are guides to the resources of the individual library: those that survey specific subjects, those that cover the several disciplines encompassed in the area studies programs now offered at many universities, and those that describe such special types of material as archives, maps, prints, and other nonbook forms. What coverage does each of these types currently provide?

In 1938, we possessed no complete national guide to our major research holdings, and this remains true in 1970. Probably the most ambitious attempt to create such a research instrument took place during the five-year period, 1927 to 1932, as a part of Project "B"—the expansion of the National Union Catalog with funds provided by John D. Rockefeller, Jr. At the end of the grant the index described and located 4,884 collections; subsequently, the Union Catalog Division continued to incorporate additional information, but was unable to do so on a basis that was systematic and encompassed regular reporting.[6] The index now contains over 7,500 entries. Although at one time it probably offered the best available information on special collections, the index never appeared in published form and is now so incomplete and outdated that one could consider it only one of the foundations—almost a kind of preliminary checking edition—on which such a guide might be constructed. Downs himself proposed the preparation of such a volume, but the necessary funds were not forthcoming. In the meantime, three editions (1958, 1961, and 1967) of Lee Ash's *Subject Collections* have appeared, but since this compilation includes all sizes and types of libraries, it lists collections of but slight importance for the scholar. Enumerative rather than descriptive, this compilation might, in fact, have been entitled *Directory of Subject Collections*. Similarly, the two editions (1963 and 1968) of A. T. Krazas' *Directory of Special Libraries and Information Centers* offer some data on resources. An attempt to provide a descriptive guide to significant current acquisitions of American research libraries resulted in a series of articles, "Notable Materials Added to American Libraries," for the years 1938–1939 through 1948–1949. Six reports (the first three by Downs), covering from one to five years each, were published in eight parts in *Library Quarterly*. Data for the five years following the last report (i.e., 1950 through 1954) were collected but not published. Since no attempt has been made to obtain information for the subsequent period, it appears that even in the unlikely event of a revival of the series there would be a twenty-year lacuna. Perhaps the articles were never fully appreciated; certainly, it appears that publication in serial form and the lack of an index made the compilation less useful than it might have been.

As we have already seen, Downs' pioneering effort in preparing a guide to resources for the southern region appeared in 1938. Five years later a similar investigation by John Van Male resulted in coverage for another area (*Resources of Pacific Northwest Libraries*), but holdings of other regions remain undescribed. (In the early years of the Midwest Interlibrary Center—now Center for Research Libraries—the possibility of such a guide for that area came under discussion.) In 1968 T. H. English's *Roads to Research; Distinguished Library Collections of the Southeast* appeared, providing more recent descriptions (generally from one to three pages) of resources in the area. Since it gives information on only fifty-one individual collections or areas of subject strength and since it covers the eastern part of the geographic area of the 1938 study, it must be viewed as only a partial updating of that work. However, it is the most recent study on the regional level.

The individual states have fared little better—at least in percentage of the fifty covered. Monographic works for Connecticut, Missouri, North Carolina, South Carolina, and Texas[7] have appeared since 1965. The Missouri, North Carolina, and Texas studies generally follow the same approach and utilize similar techniques. Each of them contains an annotated list of special collections in the state (about 140 for Missouri, 110 for North Carolina, and 250 for Texas[8]). The Connecticut volume is enumerative, while that for South Carolina has a descriptive portion and a union list of serials. In addition, a study of holdings of the four regional library resource centers of Pennsylvania[9] (Carnegie Library of Pittsburgh, Free Library of Philadelphia, Pennsylvania State University, and the State Library) might fall into the category of a partial state guide, because it omits not only such major university collections as those of Pennsylvania, Pittsburgh, and Temple, but also the Library Company of Philadelphia and the host of important libraries of colleges and newly emerging universities (several of which exceed 250,000 volumes, according to the latest edition of the *American Library Directory*).

Among the cities, New York and Washington have fared the best, although there are few descriptive guides. The Downs study, *Resources of New York City Libraries*, another forerunner in the field, now suffers from the fact that it appeared nearly three decades ago. However, the New York Chapter of the Special Libraries Association has provided more current information on an enumerative basis in the successive issues of its *Special Libraries Directory of Greater New York* (11th edition, 1967), and it is not inconceivable that the activities pertaining to resources of the New York Metropolitan Reference and Research Library Agency (METRO) might lead to one complete guide or various partial ones to the area's resources. Seven editions (from 1943 to 1966) of *Library and Reference Facilities in the Area of the District of Columbia*, prepared by the Loan Division of the Library of Congress, have provided, *faute-de-mieux*, some data on Washington's resources on a reasonably current basis, as have the directories compiled by other SLA chapters for such cities as Baltimore, Boston, Chicago, Philadelphia, and Pittsburgh.

As already mentioned, the description of an individual library's holdings constitutes still another type of guide. For this group the situation is the same as for guides on the state or city level: relatively few major libraries have had their resources adequately pictured in volumes designed for that purpose. It is true, however, that histories of individual institutions frequently contain information on the development of their collections, and by 1959 more than 130 such writings had appeared.[10] In some cases, this takes the form of a single chapter devoted to the collection, but in others the discussion of resources is scattered through various sections of a chronological account. But the history functions inadequately as a guide because, by its very nature, it emphasizes the development (and circumstances surrounding such events) rather than the present status of holdings. Among our major research libraries there is much variation in both the number and nature of publications about their resources. Our three largest collections, for example, illustrate these differences. The Library of Congress has fared poorly insofar as it lacks any overall guide to its vast holdings. As partial substitutes one can turn only to two very brief publications: the *Report on Certain Collections* (1942) and Shirley Pearlove's *Guide to Special Book Collections in the Library of Congress* (1949). From 1943 to date, the pages of the Library's *Quarterly Journal* have carried hundreds of articles (many of them reports of current acquisitions) dealing in whole or in part with specific portions of the collections, and some of the library's many other publications (e.g., the recent *Poland in the Collections of the Library of Congress*) also provide information on resources. As a result of the lack of even an index or guide to the specific data within this wealth of material, however, the user faces the tedious task of scanning vast quantities of print.

Harvard has been more fortunate. The fourth edition (1934) of Potter's *Library of Harvard University* provides descriptions of many special collections. But it appeared when holdings amounted to about 3,600,000 volumes in contrast to over 8,000,000 in 1970. Some more recent data are available in Metcalf and Williams' article "Harvard's Book Collections"[11] and Rene Kuhn Bryant's *Harvard University Library* (1969). From 1949 to 1961, and again from its revival in 1964, the *Harvard Library Bulletin* has carried a number of articles shedding light on resources, especially those on special collections or units of the library system. G. K. Hall has issued catalogs of several Harvard libraries, but the most significant key to Harvard's holdings on a current basis consists of computer printouts of sections of the Widener shelflist. More than twenty-two volumes covering such diverse subjects as Africa, Latin American literature, American history, education, bibliography, and Canadian history and literature have appeared since the series began in 1965. Because of their classified approach, these volumes permit the reader to scan sections and to draw conclusions on the overall nature of holdings as well as to locate specific titles.

At the New York Public Library we find still another story, because it is the only one of the country's three largest libraries to have a full-scale guide to its resources: the monumental volume by Karl Brown, *A Guide to the Reference Collections of the New York Public Library*, published in 1941 after being issued serially in the *Bulletin* over the previous five years. This volume has remained a standard reference and bibliographic tool, although obviously losing currency as the years passed. Discussions about a supplement or new edition did not bear fruit until 1965, when the library embarked upon the preparation of a new guide to its resources, which despite some differences in approach retains the same general purpose as Brown. By mid-1970 the manuscript was completed, with publication to come the following year. The new guide may also point the way for similar volumes on other major libraries; at least such a proposal has recently come before the ALA Committee on Resources. In the thirty years that elapsed between the two guides, two types of supplementary data were available: articles in the *Bulletin* —although in recent years it has contained relatively more on literary history and criticism and relatively less on the library's collections (early volumes had included many complete listings of holdings on specific subjects)—and, perhaps even more useful, the published reproductions of the catalogs of many of the library's major divisions. The first of these appeared in 1959, and since then G. K. Hall has issued or scheduled for publication sixteen titles, which will provide over 250 volumes of author/title/subject information.

Thus, while it is accurate to say that as of mid-1970 a current guide is not available for any of the three institutions, all have been relatively active in publishing information on their holdings. It is interesting to note that each library's journal has not served as frequently as it might have as the medium for disseminating resource information about portions of the collection—an activity to which a serial would lend itself very well. The New York Public Library and Harvard have followed similar routes in allowing modern technology to make available to the scholarly world in general tools originally prepared for internal use (divisional catalogs and the shelflist, respectively), but the Library of Congress does not seem to have adopted such a policy, except through the publication of the *Library of Congress Catalog: Books—Subjects*. This listing suffers from the semantics of subject headings and, furthermore, covers only the period since 1950. Would it also be useful to have the complete LC Shelflist available in published form as a classified approach to the collections? The Shelflist now covers more than 8,000,000 volumes in the library's classified collections,[12] and one recent resources study did make extensive use of certain sections to analyze the library's monographic holdings.

The postwar years witnessed publication of few guides to the resources of other major institutions. In the early 1950s Yale undertook to prepare such a volume but, although portions were drafted, neither the full guide nor sections of it ever appeared in print. Several annual reports of the Yale University Library do, however, provide brief descriptions of special collections.[13] Somewhat unusual is the case of the University of North Carolina, for which there are two guides. C. E. Rush's *Library Resources of the University of North Carolina* appeared in 1945, and twelve years later the Library issued its *Guide to Special Collections, Indexes and Catalogs* . . . in looseleaf, mimeograph form so that it could receive additions and revisions. In general, the lack of full-scale guides forces the person seeking information to turn to the serial publications of major libraries. To the long-established journals of such institutions as the Library of Congress, and the New York Public, Harvard, Yale, Princeton, Huntington, and Rochester Libraries, one should now add those emanating from Cornell, Iowa, and Texas.

Three other types complete the eight categories of guides to resources, for individual subjects have not appeared with great frequency. One major publication, somewhat unusual in giving coverage on an international scale, is the IFLA-sponsored *Performing Arts Museums and Libraries* (1967). More often, the subject approach manifests itself in the form of the journal article dealing with one segment of a subject or a topical special collection in a given library (e.g., the French Revolution[14]). However, in recent years a new type of guide has emerged and proliferated: that which deals with resources in various subjects, all of which are related to a single geographic area. This trend, of course, reflects the growing emphasis placed on area studies in American universities since the end of World War II. Guides of varying length and detail have been compiled—for example, for Africa, Asia, Latin America (and separately for Brazil), Russia, and East Europe. Most surveys of types of material deal with manuscript holdings, although there are publications that cover maps, archives, microfilms, prints, and photographs. Of outstanding importance is the publication in the past decade of the volumes of the *National Union Catalog of Manuscript Collections*.[15]

In reviewing the status of published guides to resources over the past three decades, one cannot fail to be struck by the fact that, despite the large number of publications relating to resources that appeared during the period, the number of guides (in the sense used in this paper) was actually small. Although one can only speculate on the reasons for this situation, there seems little doubt that lack of financial support has been a major contributing cause. While we have few indications of the cost of earlier guides, both the steady growth of library holdings (and particularly of special collections) and the general increase in library costs (notably personnel) have made the preparation of a guide to resources a larger financial commitment than it formerly was. Research libraries, already under rather severe financial pressure, have been unwilling to utilize their own funds for such projects, and foundations have apparently not wished to provide subsidy. Table I does show grants that provided aid for eleven studies in resources—seven of them guides, and four (three, if one considers the two Downs volumes a single project) other types of publications. With the exception of the Missouri and North Carolina volumes (both of which benefitted from federal funds), these grants did not provide full support for the projects. The authors' institutions in the remaining cases contributed significantly by allowing the writers leave and also, in some instances, providing secretarial assistance, supplies, and the like. Consequently, it becomes difficult to ascertain accurately the complete cost of a guide to resources. Moreover, since even the totals which we have for the Missouri and North Carolina guides represent funds provided in the mid-1960s, they would now have to be increased considerably to allow for the subsequent inflation. Although the Old Dominion Foundation's grant to the New York Public Library was intended to provide full funding for the project, as the time necessary for the research and writing extended, it became apparent that

TABLE I

GRANTS FOR ELEVEN STUDIES OF LIBRARY RESOURCES[a]

TITLE OF PUBLICATION	AMOUNT OF GRANT	SOURCE OF GRANT
Guides to resources		
Guide to the Research Collections of the New York Public Library[b]	$ 40,200	Old Dominion Foundation
Research Materials in South Carolina	6,775	South Carolina State Library; South Carolina Library Association
Resources of Missouri Libraries	25,000	Missouri State Library (federal funds)
Resources of North Carolina Libraries	30,000	North Carolina State Library (federal funds)
Resources of Texas Libraries	8,500	Coordinating Board, Texas College and University System; Texas State Library
Roads to Research	12,000	Mary Reynolds Babcock Foundation
Russian and East European Publications in Libraries of the United States	2,940	Council on Library Resources
Other resources publications		
American Library Resources, A Bibliographical Guide	3,500	Rockefeller Foundation
American Library Resources, A Bibliographical Guide, Supplement	2,000	Council on Library Resources
National Union Catalog of Manuscript Collections	370,565	Council on Library Resources
Union List of Serials, 3d ed.	269,977	Council on Library Resources
	$771,457	

[a] Sources: Annual reports of foundations indicated; unpublished data from state libraries of Missouri, North Carolina, South Carolina, and Texas.

[b] Not yet published.

the grant funds would be insufficient for completing the guide. Rather than abandoning the study or completing it only partially, the library then assumed many costs by using regular budget funds for salaries and benefits for project staff, by declining to charge the project with the customary overhead, and by accepting, in the final stages, the contributed services of the part-time project director.

The major cost for a guide to resources consists of expenditures for professional personnel because the preparation is a time-consuming process requiring at least one experienced person with a broad background. Indeed, the ultimate value of the guide may depend upon securing the relatively expensive services of just such a person or persons. Publication probably represents the next greatest cost, although there is considerable variation here, depending on such factors as whether letterpress or offset is used, whether copies are bound or paperback, whether they will be sold or distributed gratis, and whether royalty payments are made. Supplies, photocopy services, postage, telephone, etc., amount to relatively small sums, but they are essential if best use is to be made of personnel. Travel costs are almost nil in the case of the guide to a single library or those in the same city (unless the author comes from another area and makes repeated trips), but they can be considerable for projects involving various libraries in a state, regional, or national project. In all cases, secretarial and subprofessional assistance is desirable throughout the project and essential, of course, in preparing the final manuscript.

Still another problem area centers around the methodology to use in preparing the guide to resources. There is little agreement on either the techniques to apply in obtaining data or the way to describe holdings clearly. Among the various techniques utilized are the following: the questionnaire (often used when it is necessary to obtain information from various libraries at a distance from each other but often failing to provide in-depth information); measurement of shelflists and counts of volumes on the shelves to secure quantitative data; analysis of shelflist cards and subject entries in catalogs to ascertain the nature and range of titles in the collection; review of serial holdings for number of titles and completeness of files; checking of bibliographies; comparison with published data on other libraries; study of nonbook holdings; and the direct examination of volumes on the shelves. Most surveys employ a combination of these techniques. When collected, all factual data must be digested and recast into a descriptive style, which avoids both the too general statement (e.g., "holdings are ample" or "all authors are represented") and the too specific (e.g., the listing of large numbers of titles).

Since the new guide to the New York Public Library holdings represents the most recent attempt to describe the resources of a very large library, it may be of interest to summarize the methodology followed in its preparation. The basic decision was to utilize as much as possible of Karl Brown's work. In order to supplement this for the period from 1940 to the mid-1960s, it was obvious that the most efficient first step would be to locate and assemble material published since the appearance of the Brown volume. A literature search for published references to the library's research collections was undertaken. This included not only review of the library's own publications, but also of all other types of publications in the field (including those that mention NYPL holdings along with those of other libraries).

A second major activity was to establish a "Resources File" to bring together material about the research collections. This file, arranged broadly by Dewey Decimal Classification, contains full journal articles (especially those from the *Bulletin*) and selected pages from monographic studies, as well as copies of memoranda and other documents prepared for internal use. These two files, while essential to the project, represent useful additions to the library's bibliographic instruments, and new material continues to be added.

Another step was to secure up-to-date figures on the distribution of the collection by subject. A sampling technique for both volumes shelved in fixed order and for those in the general stacks and elsewhere in the library produced statistics for eighty subject categories, including the geographic approach for history of major countries and language divisions for major literatures; most other headings tended to reflect academic disciplines.

Although describing adequately the resources for each discipline posed special problems and requirements, the following steps were common to nearly all:

1. Study and critical review of the description in the Brown volume.
2. Examination of standard bibliographies and guides to the literature of the field.
3. Review of material in the Resources File and bibliographic citations for clues on general strengths and special features, especially for changed emphases or improvements in resources in the years elapsed since the Brown study.

4. Examination of the collection on the shelves.
5. Study of selected subject entries in the Public Catalog.
6. Consultation with the staff of the division having primary responsibility for the development of resources in the area and use of the division's special indexes and files.
7. Investigation of holdings of other divisions (e.g., Spencer, Slavonic, Rare Book, Manuscript) to see the extent to which their resources strengthen or supplement the main body of material.

One needs to remember that not only the complexities of dealing with large bodies of material (some of it in the more exotic foreign languages) but also the physical dispersion of resources within the Main Building (and, for certain subjects, in the Annex and in the Research Library of the Performing Arts) made this a time-consuming task. Choosing to describe resources on subjects rather than material in divisions of the Billings classification (thus reflecting physical location) was inevitably a slower technique than Brown's following that classification, but one which would better serve the library user who generally concerns himself with a subject field. Indeed, with about half of the library's new acquisitions going into fixed-order location, it would no longer have been possible to survey adequately many parts of the collection from the shelf arrangement of items in the Billings classes.

It is clear from the experience gained in this study that the preparation of a guide to the resources of a major research library has become a large and complex undertaking. It is not something that can be done in a routine fashion, nor can it be based on statistical techniques alone. It is also apparent that such a project requires several man/years of work, even though the use of a team might shorten the elapsed time. Certain preliminary operations (e.g., a literature search), while time-consuming at the outset, do represent long-range economies in the use of staff. The expenditure to prepare such a guide will probably approach $100,000 and could be higher depending on the amount of in-depth analysis desired. Extensive checking of bibliographies, for example, will greatly increase costs.

This article has discussed the development of the guide to research resources over the past generation. This type of publication has established itself as an important form within the literature of librarianship.

While it is true that guides are expensive projects to undertake, they make a real contribution to the world of learning by increasing the availability of information about collections to the students, scholars, and researchers who will use them.

References

1. Robert B. Downs, *Resources of Southern Libraries* (Chicago: American Library Association, 1938), p. xi.
2. Robert B. Downs, "Research in Problems of Resources," *Library Trends* VI (1957–1958): 147–159.
3. Edwin E. Williams, "Surveying Library Collections," *in* Maurice F. Tauber and Irlene Roemer Stephens, eds., *Library Surveys* (Columbia University Studies in Library Service, no. 16; New York: Columbia University Press, 1967), pp. 25–27.
4. Robert B. Downs, *American Library Resources, A Bibliographical Guide* (Chicago: American Library Association, 1951), p. 1.
5. Louis R. Wilson *et al.*, *The Library in College Instruction* (New York: H. W. Wilson, 1951), p. 57.
6. George A. Schwegmann, "The National Union Catalog in the Library of Congress," *in* Robert B. Downs, ed., *Union Catalogs in the United States* (Chicago: American Library Association, 1942), pp. 231, 245–246.
7. Charles E. Funk, Jr., ed., *Directory of Subject Strengths in Connecticut Libraries* (Hartford: Connecticut State Library, 1968); Robert B. Downs, ed., *Resources of Missouri Libraries* (Jefferson City: Missouri State Library, 1966); Robert B. Downs, ed., *Resources of North Carolina Libraries* (Raleigh: Governor's Commission on Library Resources, 1965); John H. Moore, *Research Materials in South Carolina: A Guide* (Columbia: University of South Carolina Press, 1967); Edward G. Holley and Donald D. Hendricks, *Resources of Texas Libraries* (Austin: Field Services Division, Texas State Library, 1968).
8. Robert B. Downs, *Resources of Missouri Libraries*, pp. 135–156; Robert B. Downs, *Resources of North Carolina Libraries*, pp. 177–190; Holley and Hendricks, *Resources of Texas Libraries*, pp. 274–334.
9. Ralph W. McComb, *Guide to the Resources of the Regional Library Resource Centers of Pennsylvania* (Harrisburg: Department of Public Instruction, 1967).
10. Harry Bach, "Bibliographical Essay on the History of Scholarly Libraries in the United States, 1800 to the Present," University of Illinois Graduate School of Library Science, *Occasional Papers*, no. 54 (January, 1959).
11. *Harvard Library Bulletin* V (1951): 51–62, 209–220.
12. U.S. Library of Congress, *Annual Report of the Librarian of Congress for the Fiscal Year Ending June 30, 1969* (Washington: U.S. Govt. Print. Off., 1970), Appendix 3, p. 109.
13. Yale University, *Report of the Librarian, July 1960–June 1961*, pp. 33–105; *ibid.*, *1965–1966*, pp. 36–95.
14. Maria Ann Haubold, "The French Revolution Collection," *Books at Iowa* no. 3 (November, 1965): 5–9.

15. For a listing of representative guides arranged by these eight types, see William V. Jackson, *Resources of Research Libraries, A Selected Bibliography* (Pittsburgh: University of Pittsburgh Book Center, 1969), pp. 11–24.

About the Author

William V. Jackson is now teaching in two fields at the Joint University in Nashville, Tennessee. He is a Professor in Library Service at Peabody and Professor of Spanish and Portuguese at Vanderbilt. His first contact with Downs was in 1950 when he entered the Library School at Illinois. His great interest in resources dates from that time. He has taught and traveled extensively in the interest of library development and resources, mainly in Latin America but also in Europe. Frequently a consultant for the State Department and AID, he is highly regarded for his work as a teacher and bibliographer.

COLLECTION BUILDING AND RARE BOOKS

by Robert Vosper

The powerful and steady growth of book collections in individual American university libraries, particularly during the mid-twentieth century, has been a major achievement in American cultural and educational history. It has both matched and fostered the ebullient and questing intellectual life of the universities themselves, and it has been a marvel to many foreign observers.

The Report of the Shackleton Committee on University Libraries at Oxford, issued in 1966, has this to say: "Oxford's library expenditure, large though it is in comparison with the expenditure of most other British universities, is still considerably less than the expenditure in a large number of American university libraries. A remarkable feature of American universities since the war has been the unfaltering growth of even the largest libraries. This can be seen both in the rate of book acquisition and in the rate of expenditure. Such comparisons are disheartening. It is a national disgrace that British university libraries are so starved of money for books. Indeed it can be demonstrated that the present state of most university libraries constitutes a national emergency."

Although the Report of the Parry Committee on Libraries, presented in 1967 to its parent body, the British Government's University Grants Committee, is not so pungent in tone, it does at several points indicate with distress the disparity between the British and American university libraries in terms of financial support, total size of collections, and richness of current intake.

Outside observers are equally struck by the considerable numbers of American university libraries that, in a relatively short lifetime, have achieved levels of distinction and vitality. Yet it can be said, fairly, that the phenomenon of rapid numerical growth in holdings as well as qualitative growth in breadth and depth is exemplified particularly in such eminent state universities as Illinois, Michigan, Berkeley, and Cornell (the last, to be sure, a partially private institution) since, except for Michigan, they are barely a century old. Thus they confirm the ambitious commitment of a pioneering American society to a new view of higher education as being tax supported and thereby broadly available to aspiring young people, and as being devoted at once to traditional academic excellence as well as to the unique new conceptions of the Morrill Act of 1862 (again except for Michigan).

Not only does each of these libraries today have total collections rapidly exceeding the three and four million volume range (by way of the annual intake of well over 150,000 volumes and the regular receipt of 35,000 or more serials), but all are unquestionably judged by scholars to be qualitatively among the greatest research libraries of the world and of high distinction in a wide range of disciplines (historical ones and those concerned with contemporary scientific and social problems).

It should be noted that the university libraries mentioned above are nearly equaled in these levels of excellence by a number of others, including Indiana, Minnesota, UCLA, and Wisconsin. Berkeley's East Asiatic Library is one of the greatest of its kind in the world. The collections of original works in the history of science at Wisconsin and Cornell are exceeded no doubt by those at Harvard but hardly matched elsewhere. Perhaps nowhere else, not even in Great Britain, would a scholar find in one place so rich a Milton collection as at Illinois or so extensive a collection of nineteenth century English fiction as at UCLA. Indiana's Lilly Library, Berkeley's Bancroft, Michigan's Clements, and UCLA's Clark are all, in their fields of concentration, probably *non pareil.*

These are but examples of peaks of highest eminence which come readily to mind; an inventory would reveal many others. But the most striking thing about these great modern state university libraries is the diverse and extensive range of disciplines in which each library supports research with impressive collections as well as lively services. In this wide-ranging and optimistic approach to knowledge these state university libraries, of course, reflect, interact with, and even at times stimulate their parent universities, which are of an omnibus intellectual style that hardly exists outside this country and Canada. Each year hundreds of PhD candidates in scores of fields find in their own institutions a sufficiency of published material, and even manuscripts, to support their dissertations. In each of these libraries large numbers of the world's greatest scholars can conduct seminars and pursue research, often in highly abstruse areas of knowledge, with but occasional or tangential reference to other libraries. The frame of reference is virtually unlimited as to historical time, language, or geography. Each of these libraries is indeed a phenomenal institution.

Yet despite the obvious successes of these libraries and despite the admitted envy with which they are often viewed from outside, their librarians have long known, as have all thoughtful academic librarians, that the concept of the self-sufficient all-encompassing library is only a myth—although a myth which many of their scholarly clientele would still hold as truth. Faced with this realization, the American research library community has forcefully undertaken a number of imaginative, voluntary joint actions that would supplement the capabilities of individual libraries, particularly through national programs, and thus enhance overall service to scholarship.

The goal of the Farmington Plan as originally conceived in 1942 and initiated in 1948, under the auspices of the Association of Research Libraries, was the development of a continuing, voluntary, cooperative national system for resource development concentrating broadly on foreign publications. At least as early as the 1920s American library leaders had proposed the ideal of "providing somewhere, somehow, in American libraries, at least one copy of every book that may be needed for research." The Farmington Plan, stemming from the critical experiences of the Second World War, picked up that ideal and has been pursuing it ever since, under the leadership of such eminent librarians as Keyes Metcalf of Harvard and Robert B. Downs of Illinois. In the national interest, a large number of libraries (over fifty today) agreed to accept individual responsibility for specified subject fields, and at a later date for specified geographical areas, within which they would receive, catalog, and make available comprehensive collections of currently published foreign books. It was understood definitely that in the fields or areas so selected the individual library would be receiving, and in fact paying for, a far richer intake of secondary or peripheral publications than required by its local clientele. However, since in intention all fields of knowledge and all countries were eventually to be so covered by the plan, the division of labor was expected to assure American scholars in general of a far more extensive pool of research material than could ever be achieved on an uncoordinated, laissez-faire basis.

This cooperative approach at the national level was given particular impetus and meaning through a crucial statement in 1945 by Archibald MacLeish, then Assistant Secretary of State and formerly the Librarian of Congress, "that the national interest is affected" by the collective holdings of American research libraries. That generous statement opened up a whole new era of American academic librarianship and set a tone that has been heard with increasing clarity over the subsequent years.

In practice, the Farmington Plan can be faulted in many details, and it has been subject to persistent criticism and analysis from outside as well as from within the system. One British critic pungently called it "a large, costly and rather clumsy sledge-hammer to crack so small a nut." Some European librarians, committed to the classical pattern of building research library collections neatly book by book, have been especially critical of its gross selection method. Farmington participants themselves have persistently debated the tough and fundamental question of how one effectively decides which currently published books "might reasonably be expected to be of interest to a research worker in America." Moreover, to many librarians the operation of the plan was slow to move forward; for many years it was limited virtually to western Europe and almost solely to "trade" books.

However, considered from this point in time it is probably fair to say that in operating terms alone the Farmington Plan has been a remarkable undertaking. Its concept was both generous and foresighted. When one thinks of the number of independent libraries involved and the variety of their jurisdictions (national libraries, private university libraries, state university libraries of different sizes and wealth, and some large municipal libraries); the number of countries and contractual book agencies involved; the intricate technical and intellectual details; and particularly the fact of its voluntary nature, dependent wholly on the financial support of the participating libraries; then it can be described as a powerful and perhaps unique instrumentality with but minor mechanical imperfections. Furthermore, as its most thorough assessment indicated in 1959, the Farmington Plan should be viewed and weighed not as a particular mechanism for book procurement at the national level but as an intention. In these terms, although even today far from the ideal goal, the Farmington Plan can only be applauded.

When in the later 1950s American higher education, with the encouragement of the federal government, moved massively into interdisciplinary foreign-area study programs concerned with all parts of the globe, and especially with those areas previously of little concern to American scholarship, the mechanism and experience of the Farmington Plan was available for immediate use. Its administration was sufficiently flexible to enable libraries to respond to the complex new requirements with commendable efficiency and speed. This same urgent new interest in foreign-area study programs also gave further support to the importance of acquiring secondary and peripheral publications because these are the raw materials for studies in social history and development.

It is worth noting that some of the earlier criticisms leveled against the Farmington Plan by foreign librarians have been modified by more recent attitudes toward research, particularly in the social sciences. The Parry Report, mentioned earlier, specifies that "we regard as essential that all foreign publications likely to be of value to scholars should be readily found in a British library." The 1969 Report of the National Libraries Committee (the "Dainton" Committee) to Parliament says specifically that, "the social scientist is interested not only in published monographs, periodicals and reports, but also in a great quantity and variety of ephemeral material which is, nevertheless, important as primary material for research."

Furthermore, based as the Farmington Plan was in the MacLeish doctrine of "the national interest" the Association of Research Libraries was in a strong position by the 1960s to forge closer and closer links with the Federal Government in the design of national library policy and funding. Federal involvement then is the theme of that decade and the promise of the 1970s.

The first step forward, becoming operational in 1960, was the use of counterpart funds, under the Dingell Amendment to Public Law 480, for the purchase of library materials in certain countries where the U.S. Treasury had declared funds to be surplus. This fostered the receipt by selected libraries of rich stocks of publications from such countries as the United Arab Republic, India and Pakistan, Israel, and Yugoslavia. Thus, in a limited way, the principle of direct federal fiscal support for the growth of American research library collections was established. The complicated linguistic and cataloging problems stemming from this massive intake of publications in relatively obscure languages thereupon gave the Association of Research Libraries a sound basis for discussing the concept of "Shared Cataloging" as a matter of national interest with key members of the Congress and other Federal officials.

From these discussions there evolved with dramatic speed the epoch-making Title II-C of the Higher Education Act of 1965. Under Title II-C, the Library of Congress is provided with authorization and funding for: "(1) acquiring, so far as possible, all library materials currently published throughout the world which are of value to scholarship; and (2) providing catalog information for these materials promptly after receipt and distributing bibliographic information by printing cards and other means."

The evolutive relationship of this new Library of Congress mission, appropriately called the National Program for Acquisitions and Cataloging (NPAC), to the Farmington experience and to the doctrine of the "national interest" is clear. The speed and precision with which this extensive, global program was put into action by the Library of Congress and other participants deserves forthright praise. Essential to that success was the operational overseas experience of Farmington and of the Public Law 480 program.

It would be burdensome here to describe other large-scale structures established by joint action of American research libraries to effect collection building at the national level on top of local bases—such structures as the Center for Research Libraries, the Current Foreign Newspaper Microfilming Project of the Association of Research Libraries, that Association's new Center for Chinese Research Materials, and its Slavic Bibliographic and Documentation Center. Instead of an inventory of such projects, what must be surely noted here is the persistence of the trend and the vitality of the effort.

Not to be overlooked as between the local and national levels of collection development are some of the more recent attempts within a few state systems (New York State and Illinois, for example) and certain smaller regional groups (such as the Chapel Hill–Durham–Raleigh area) at a better rationalization of acquisitions planning and service to users within such areas. However, it is much too soon to judge the overall and continuing significance of these efforts. What is clear is that with increasing talk, often rather faddish, about library networks, consortia, and regional systems, we need more precise evaluations to guide future planning, particularly with reference to the points of advantage and disadvantage as between national efforts and regional or state efforts. It is a matter of some interest that the Midwest Inter-Library Center, established in 1949 as a regional consortium, was reconstituted in 1965 as the Center for Research Libraries with a national mission. Yet at this very time the National Library of Medicine, under new authorization, began to develop a system of regional medical libraries across the country.

METHOD

This dramatic growth, in size and quality, of individual university libraries has, of course, been the result of an optimistic, even aggressive—and some would go so far as to say "piratical"—approach to collection building on the part of both scholars and their librarians. Book selection has generally been on a wholesale and opportunistic basis rather than proceeding from classical selection policies or criteria involving a precise evaluation of the worth of each book. As J. P. Danton pointed out in his *Book Selection and Collections,* an illuminating comparison of German and American university library practices, this American style of collection building is in full contrast with the long-standing tradition of academic librarianship in Germany. Whereas the American style has been gross and accumulative, the German style has been carefully designed and engineered to assure a rigorous review of the fundamental scholarly importance of each book added to the collections. One could perhaps relate this sharp difference in professional style to certain obvious national characteristics, but more particular factors can be suggested at least. American universities themselves have operated within a competitive, laissez-faire system, wherein distinguished faculty members are attracted from one institution to another by higher salaries (there being no standard national scale) and also by promises of forcefully developed book collections. One recognized measure of prestige among universities has been this very matter of aggressive library growth; thus, when the American Council on Education issued *An Assessment of Quality in Graduate Education* in 1966, there was included a careful rating of libraries—with particular attention to total size of collections and the richness of the current intake of both books and journals—because "no other single nonhuman factor is as closely related to the quality of graduate education."

The American tradition of libraries and of education in general, including higher education, has emphasized the values inherent in local control and autonomy rather than centralized direction or pattern setting through a system of strong national ministries, as in Europe, or even such a moderating body as the British University Grants Committee. The strength of this open American system, if it can be called a system, has been in terms of diversity and variety as well as in the encouragement for change, experimentation, and growth that is fostered by competition. Yet the evidence of wastefulness and low capacity for long-term planning has been sufficient in very recent years to force a noticeable shift, for both higher education and libraries in general, toward greater national participation in both planning and financing.

Economics has assuredly been another factor in the American style of collection building, for until quite recently and during the Great Depression years, American academic librarians have operated in a bullish economy, assuming and arguing for continually expanding book funds. Universities themselves have proceeded on the assumption of a steadily increasing public and private investment in higher education. Only very recently have these assumptions been seriously questioned, and only very recently has it been generally agreed that the federal government must bear a larger and larger share of the costs of education and of libraries with all the hazards of control and interference that this may involve.

The very style of scholarship in American universities has also been a significant factor in the style of collection building. In contrast with the British experience, which until quite recently has given relatively little attention to research or to graduate (doctoral) and professional education, American universities for the past century, and with a powerful impetus in the years following the Second World War, have greatly emphasized these activities. The emphasis occurs, moreover, in large numbers of institutions serving extensive populations of faculty and graduate students, as well as research workers in industry and government. The consequent pressure for mushrooming library collections has been great. Another influential aspect of American scholarship, alluded to earlier, has been the long-standing concern with the newer disciplines and, particularly, the social sciences, including the social aspects of historical and literary studies. For at least two generations, for example, American historians have wanted ready access to newspaper files, as one body of evidence, and literary scholars have wanted access to "popular" literature as well as to classical landmarks. All of this has been, at least until quite recently, in contrast with the European and British traditions of respectable scholarship.

Moreover, American academic librarians have been led to build their own self-sufficient local collections with relatively little attention to the availability of resources elsewhere because of the very difficulty in this country of assuring their scholars that books essential to research work can in fact be secured quickly and precisely from another source. This is partly the consequence of the size of the country and the very large population of users; it is also the consequence of inadequate tools and mechanisms for assured external access. In Germany, by contrast, the system of regional union catalogs and interlibrary lending for academic users has been remarkably efficient. And in so small a country as Great Britain, a central lending library for scientific and technical journals has been able to operate speedily and effectively.

In response then to these several stimuli, American university librarians have pursued a course of collection building that can be described, fairly, as imaginative and resourceful, often imprudent and risk-taking, and remarkably successful. All told, as an episode in bibliothecal history this experience can be compared with the widespread Renaissance search for manuscripts and the development of the great princely libraries in Italy. Moreover, many of the forceful collecting methods and attitudes of university librarians in the mid-twentieth century parallel those of the great private collectors of the nineteenth and early twentieth centuries.

A variety of urgent methods and tactics have been applied in this undertaking, over and beyond the essential, but slow and less colorful task of diligently searching out individual books. Each of these successful American libraries, and this is equally as true of the private as it is of the state universities, is studded with those rich plums, the en bloc collections that had already been carefully constructed by scholars or private collectors prior to being brought into the institutional library holdings. The librarian, working against time, against many other demands on his budget, and against the competition of his eager colleagues, but urged on and abetted by his faculty and often his administrative officers, has sought out these private libraries in the world's book market. Against equal competition he has sought them out as gifts in the homes of their collectors and in meetings of bibliophilic societies.

The Stellfeld Music Collection at Michigan, the Streeter Collection at Yale, Michael Sadleir's novels at UCLA, Indiana's Lilly Library and the Bancroft itself at Berkeley, the Mazzoni Collection at Duke, Fitzpatrick at Kansas, Mitsui Bunko at Berkeley, the Franklin J. Meine and Hollander collections at Illinois, Duveen and Thordarson at Wisconsin and Hanley at Texas, the Upton Sinclair archives at Indiana and those of Carl Sandburg and H. G. Wells at Illinois—these are but examples of the bonanzas that enterprising librarians have dug out of the book trade or the world of collectors. In fact, en bloc acquisition has been a recognized method of rapid collection building from the earliest days of many American universities. The founding presidents of Cornell and Chicago personally used this method to begin their institutional libraries, and Berkeley's purchase of Bancroft came early in its history. To be sure, however, the great flourishing of this method has come in the optimistic days of the mid-twentieth century.

Not only have entire private collections been acquired en bloc, but on occasion a quick-witted and fast-acting librarian has been able to purchase the full contents of an antiquarian dealer's catalog before competitors have picked it to pieces book by book. In general, of course, these have been highly focused catalogs, the equivalent, in a sense, of privately developed collections rather than miscellanies. Lawrence Clark Powell, the leading spokesman for the lively art of institutional book collecting as well as one of the most successful activists in the business, has written a charming essay "To Newbury to Buy an Old Book" about his negotiations to purchase H. W. Edwards' stock of Protestant Theology as soon as the first of a projected series of catalogs was issued. The extensive Winston Churchill Collection at Illinois came by way of the outright purchase of one of Harold Mortlake's recent catalogs. A dramatic example of this forthright method of library collection building was the purchase in 1969 for Brigham Young University by a generous alumnus, of David Magee's 3,000-volume collection of Victorian literature and Victoriana. In this instance the principals so neatly dovetailed their efforts that when the initial two volumes of the intended three-volume Magee catalog appeared, a printed notice about the sale was inserted.

However, even these one-shot acquisitive efforts are dwarfed by the occasional decision of a librarian not to buy just a dealer's cataloged collection but, boa-like, to absorb his complete book stock. In 1968, Kent State University bought up Gilman's 250,000-volume stock, and in 1970, Pennsylvania State's purchase of the Aberdeen Book Company's holdings involved twice that many books. In these cases, relatively young or rapidly expanding libraries could justify the purchase of such large generalist accumulations, from which at a low unit cost they might expect to select the large numbers of common but essential books that older libraries would have acquired piecemeal over the years.

In a slightly different mode, in 1963, a generous friend in the local community enabled UCLA to purchase outright the 35,000-volume holdings of an antiquarian shop in Jerusalem specializing in scholarly Hebraica and Judaica. The firm of Bamberger and Wahrman came up for sale on the death of the last surviving partner, and thus the UCLA Library was able quickly to give heart to a new but aspiring program of Hebrew studies. Somewhat similarly, Texas recently acquired all of Weinreb's specialist stock in architectural history.

The Indiana University Foundation's takeover of the corporate stock of the Lathrop C. Harper firm during 1967–1968 was a far more sophisticated undertaking than any of these others. Yet in a way, the University of British Columbia Library in 1967 topped these several avaricious enterprises by absorbing not only thirty-six tons of Mr. Norman Colbeck's private stock, but even Mr. Colbeck himself, who left Bournemouth for Vancouver to join the Library's staff. The coming of Mr. David Randall, who had been Mr. J. K. Lilly's primary agent, to head up the Lilly Library when it was generously implanted at the University of Indiana by the collector, is of a quite different style from the indenture of Mr. Colbeck.

The UBC coup reminds us that in very recent years some of the Canadian provincial university libraries, Alberta and Toronto as well as British Columbia, have been powerful competitors to their American colleagues in this collection building business. This might also be the place for another parenthetical remark, to the effect that some of the separately established American research libraries, as well as the university libraries, have been less than reticent in their collection building, as witness the Folger's purchase of the Harmsworth Collection in 1938 and Lawrence W. Towner's brilliant success more recently as the entrepreneurial Director of the Newberry Library.

Not only have a variety of colorful methods been applied to the acquisition of books, but the selection procedures have also varied in an interesting way. The long tradition in American university libraries, holding generally until the late 1950s, was to depend on faculty recommendations for the greatest part of book selection. The earlier professional literature is full of discussions of allocating total book funds among academic departments or fields and the consequent use of departmental committees or academic specialists for providing advice on what to buy with those allocations, whether among new books, older books, or journal subscriptions. In many cases, this was an effective mechanism, for presumably the faculty specialists like the German *Referenten* (library subject specialists), had a first-hand and precise knowledge of the bibliography of their disciplines and thus could judge the scholarly worth of each book under consideration. Moreover, in a more leisurely and less specialized academic world there were more than a few American faculty members who combined a wide-ranging bibliographic knowledge with the true book collector's zeal. For the eager junior member of the faculty opening up a new intellectual field at a young institution, and in an era when men tended to make their careers in a single institution, there was the opportunity and encouragement for acquiring the stock of books with which he could foster that career, both for himself and for his students. The earlier history of the great American university libraries can often be indexed by the names of the professors who developed specialized scholarly collections book by book, diligently reading catalogs and reviews as well as prowling through book shops when on academic leave. To the librarians was left the less dramatic task of bridging the gaps and trying somehow to make sense of the overall acquisitions effort. Increasingly, these librarians pointed out that the gaps were widening as faculty specialties narrowed or as the specialists increasingly moved to other universities, leaving behind highly developed collections with no continuing local use.

There always were, to be sure, some librarians with a highly developed sense of institutional book collecting—men such as Powell at UCLA and Nyholm at Northwestern—who not only projected an acquisitive style and pattern for the libraries they headed, but who also went personally into the book market with professional skill and bibliophilic enthusiasm. At Yale, James Babb's sensitive touch for the selection of potential donors had a major impact on that library's growth in distinction. At least two institutions—Pennsylvania and Cornell—have been blessed with senior men of an all-too-scarce type—Rudolph Hirsch and Felix Reichman—both acquisitions librarians with a European antiquarian book trade background and the almost polymathic knowledge of scholarly books which only that background can provide. At Berkeley, in the years between the two world wars, the Publications Exchange Librarian, Miss Ivander MacIver, used that bartering device with both impressive sweep and bibliographic precision to establish one of the permanent strengths of that library—its extensive files of the serial publication of foreign academies and universities.

By and large, however, selection was a faculty responsibility or prerogative until the later 1950s, when it was gradually turned over to a new breed of library staff specialists. Several factors led to this fundamental change. Faculty members became increasingly busy with research projects and involved with larger numbers of graduate students. The greater mobility of faculty members, in an age of relative affluence for higher education and research, resulted in men building their careers more within a discipline than within a particular institution. In consequence of this, faculty members were seldom around long enough to learn the strengths of a particular library or to participate wholeheartedly in the time-consuming book selection business. The increasing pace of much research, both in the social sciences and in the physical, biological, and engineering sciences, put a high premium on quick access to newly published books, with the result that libraries were pressed to find mechanisms for bringing new books in prior to the book-reviewing process. The rapid rise in the rate of publication and the enormous size of library holdings, coupled with the fact that faculty members were increasingly busy with research and teaching, made it less likely for younger men to develop wide-ranging bibliographic expertise. Another powerful factor was the burgeoning foreign area field, which required libraries to become ingenious and aggressive at securing publications, often scarce, from parts of the world where the book trade and bibliographic apparatus could not support a leisurely, classical book selection and purchase mechanism.

All of these factors, together with the increasing sophistication of many librarians, led to the development of a new type of librarian specializing in book selection. Most commonly called "bibliographers," a rather ambiguous use of the term, the best of these new selection officers bring to this task a professional understanding of library functions, a broad knowledge of bibliography and the book trade, specialized linguistic and academic competence, a close intellectual liaison with their faculty clientele, and full-time persistent attention to collection building. Admittedly not every "bibliographer" is such a paragon, for the variety of learned skills required is exacting. Yet to one degree or another most of the larger academic libraries in the country have pieced together a cadre of such specialists during the past ten to fifteen years, and the tide of book selection has pretty much ebbed away from the faculty, generally, it might be said, to the pleasure of the faculty.

Thus, American university librarianship in very recent years has taken up the tradition of the *Referatsystem* (subject field specialists) that the German academic libraries have depended on since the early twentieth century. It is to be hoped that some of the disabilities of the German experience can be avoided, most particularly the rather arrogant assumption of the *Referenten* that they alone could be the arbiters of collection building. This kind of stiff-necked attitude is of course an endemic disease of all professions, but the tragic result in Germany, as Danton has observed, was that the central libraries in many universities so lost touch with academic reality that the professors bypassed them and set up their own strong "institute" libraries. To a certain extent, a creative university library must extend above and beyond the limitations of a particular time and of a particular faculty or curriculum. Yet in terms of dynamic reality the library, at any point in time, must come close to serving the needs of the current faculty and curriculum, or it will lose support and credibility. Therefore, the American librarian should continue to strive for a mutuality of effort and of goal setting with his colleagues on the faculty.

The growing need for this new type of librarian book selector has put stresses on both the programs of library schools and the personnel structures of academic libraries. Both institutions must find more flexible procedures for attracting, training, and retaining people with an uncommon amount of academic expertise and a large measure of intellectual drive and imagination. The library must, in fact, compete with academic departments for the brightest graduate students. It must then be able to offer these people rewards and prerogatives competitive with those they could receive if they went, instead, to regular faculty appointments. In some cases, joint appointments between the library and an academic department may be the best answer, particularly in assuring mutual understanding, although any dual assignment can be stressful for the conscientious incumbent.

Two mechanisms for selection and procurement that have flourished in these recent boom days have been the field trip and the blanket order. The occasional librarian or scholar wandering through the antiquarian book markets of Great Britain and Western Europe is no new phenomenon. The Folger Library even offered the tempting example of a resident book buyer in London several years ago. With rising library affluence, greater competition for increasingly scarce books, and larger numbers of skilled librarian book selectors, the field trip became almost a standard procedure for more ambitious libraries during the 1950s and 1960s. The foreign-area study program was again a prime mover because outside of Great Britain and Western Europe, where the book trade and bibliographic apparatus are generally efficient, often the only effective way to locate publications and to develop trading relationships is at first hand in the field. Thus American "bibliographers," with cash and letter of credit in hand, spread out through Africa, the Middle East, Latin America, and Asia, knocking on the doors of government offices, itinerant publishers, local bookstores and libraries, in search of unregistered and elusive publications.

On quite the other hand, in those countries that have an established book apparatus, many large libraries have found it advantageous to adapt the Farmington use of foreign booksellers as agents, operating under blanket instructions to supply automatically, upon publication, certain specified categories of new books. This blanket-order mechanism was first used by the Library of Congress and the New York Public Library just after the war, but increasingly in the 1960s it was picked up by academic libraries as a device for getting newly published books quickly into the library in order to satisfy urgent faculty demands. The blanket order is severely criticized, as was the Farmington Plan, by those who view selection as a precise, advance judgment of each book coming into the library. Against that judgment must be weighed the advantage of rapid receipt and the further fact that in many parts of the world, Eastern Europe and Latin America among others, books go out of print so soon after publication that purchase orders based on thoughtful prior review may be quite futile. Moreover, one can make a strong case for institutional collection building as being more a matter of pattern setting and trends than of book-by-book evaluation, or at least a combination of the two approaches. Furthermore, the blanket order implies a patterned definition of categories that can be more or less rigorous and that can and should be closely monitored. If well managed, it does not involve a slipshod attitude toward collection building, and if well organized, it should reduce some of the paper work required by a purchase procedure tied to single book orders.

PROSPECTS

What does all of this heady experience suggest for the future? The year 1965 marked a high point in optimism as well as a significant watershed, with its brilliant sequence of Congressional actions, firmly guided by the Administration, in behalf of national support for the development of all types of library service. The Higher Education Act of 1965 not only instituted the National Program for Acquisitions and Cataloging under Title II-C but also, in another section, undertook for the first time to make direct grants to colleges and universities for the development of library collections. In addition the act provided for financial aid to library research and education. This was the year also of the carefully engineered

Medical Library Assistance Act, as well as other legislation in behalf of public and school libraries. It will also be remembered that in 1965 the national mission of the Center for Research Libraries was instituted. Thus, a legislative trend toward national involvement, foreshadowed as recently as 1955 with the incipient Library Services Act, seemed in a decade to have approached an apogee.

No wonder then that academic librarians were euphoric. They foresaw not only greater fiscal support for their local collection building but also, and more importantly, a sound basis for the better rationalization of such local efforts within a national program. It did look as though a number of long-standing aspirations were to be realized. A year later, President Johnson capped this optimism by appointing a temporary National Advisory Commission on Libraries, chaired by President Douglas Knight of Duke University, the first such attempt by the federal government to undertake a comprehensive appraisal of the role of libraries in the life of the nation. Academic libraries received special attention because the commission delegated to the prestigious American Council of Learned Societies particular responsibility for the appraisal of research libraries. The consequent ACLS Committee, chaired personally by the President of ACLS, Dr. Frederick Burkhardt, who was also vice-chairman of the parent commission, submitted its advice and plea by way of a small volume entitled *On Research Libraries*. Thoughtfully, and at times even eloquently, it defines the requirements and the aspirations of today's academic and other research libraries as they look to the future within the national setting.

Now, with cruel abruptness, the critical issues centering on the war in Vietnam, a new Administration in Washington, and the travail of higher education have somewhat clouded the bright crystal ball. It is certainly clear that the time scale has changed for reaching some of the goals that had seemed as close to hand as the moon and that some of the mechanisms for reaching those goals must be reconsidered. However, it seems equally clear that this recent shift toward a more rational partnership between the federal government and local or state authorities for the planning and financing of both higher education and library services is based on significant, enduring trends. It is of more than slight interest that very similar trends are concurrently evident also in Great Britain, as indicated by the several official analyses of academic and national library functions. Moreover, the long-standing persistence and extent of informed Congressional interest in library affairs can only be heartening to American librarians.

Most importantly, the Congress has now authorized a permanent National Commission on Libraries and Information Science, as proposed by the Temporary Commission and long envisioned by many thoughtful librarians. No one would expect such a body to concoct panaceas, and possible hazards can reasonably be inferred by any critical observer of national commissions in Washington. Certainly a major potential for hazard, as well as for success, will lie in the continuous search for a proper balance between central planning and local autonomy or between uniformity and variety, but this balancing act is an essential aspect of American political life. Herein lies, of course, an especially sensitive matter for higher education as well as for libraries, but perhaps we can learn something by observing the recent history of that once sacrosanct body, the British University Grants Committee.

It is not fully recognized that within the structure of the American university the library is already involved in a complexity of goal-setting relationships, as between its responsibilities to the campus community, to regional entities or consortia, and increasingly to national efforts. Thus, one of the significant problems to be dealt with as this national trend becomes clearer will be that of research library governance. Once again, a little reading on the comparative scene might be illuminating. In Italy, for example, university library policy stems from one national ministry and that for higher education from another, a simplistic severing of one Gordian knot while thereby tying others of greater intricacy.

But more urgently, in behalf of scholarship, librarians must continue to put their minds to improving existing structures and devising new ones for the proper coordination, at the national level, of research library collection development and for the assurance of ready access, bibliographically and otherwise, to those collections. Librarians must also seek the informed support of the scholarly community in this effort, and here may be the more subtle task, for much of scholarly research is necessarily a highly individualistic effort based on personal insights, experiences, and habits, which may be hard to change.

However, despite an apparent, and one would hope somewhat temporary, lack of fiscal support, both locally and nationally, a number of powerful new tools are now available or are being forged for this co-ordinating task. The full potentials of the Center for Research Libraries, as both lending and collecting mechanism, have not yet been fully tapped. At the bibliographic level, the recent appearance of the initial volumes of the published retrospective National Union Catalog is a land-mark event in library and publishing history. The first steps have also been taken toward a computerized national union list of serials, and with the advent of MARC II tapes from the Library of Congress another in-genious tool for national bibliographic control is soon to be with us. Bibliographic apparatus of these types is an essential underpinning to any effective national program of collection building. Moreover, in be-half of a better informed rapport with scholars the ACLS has now given permanent status to its Committee on Research Libraries.

Thus, it can still be said with assurance that national involvement is the promise of the 1970s. Yet even as we work at building research library collections at both the local and the national level, it is perhaps time for us to stretch our imaginations a bit further. Already, both MEDLARS and MARC bibliographic tapes are being used or experi-mented with in several other countries. The National Program for Ac-quisitions and Cataloging has not only fostered, finally, a practical shar-ing of cataloging data across national and linguistic borders; it has also established the basic structure for a global procurement system. There-fore, during this next decade we should open our minds increasingly to the implications of that pan-Scandinavian version of Farmington called the Scandia Plan, as well as to the beneficial potentials of such bodies as the International Federation of Library Associations and the International Federation for Documentation. International involvement may well be the theme and the promise of the 1980s.

Bibliography

American Council of Learned Societies. Committee on Research Libraries. *On Re-search Libraries*. Cambridge, Mass.: M.I.T. Press, 1969.

Cartter, Allan M. *An Assessment of Quality in Graduate Education.* Washington: American Council on Education, 1966.

Danton, J. P. *Book Selection and Collections: A Comparison of German and American University Libraries.* N.Y.: Columbia Univ. Press, 1963.

——— "The Subject Specialist in National and University Libraries, with Special Reference to Book Selection." *Libri* 17 (1967): 42–58.

Downs, Robert B. "Rare Books in American State University Libraries." *The Book Collector* 6 (1957): 232–243.

Great Britain. Department of Education and Science. *Report of the National Libraries Committee* (The Dainton Report). HMSO, 1969, Cmnd. 4028.

Great Britain. University Grants Committee. *Report of the Committee on Libraries* (The Parry Report). HMSO, 1967.

Hamlin, Arthur T. "The Book Collections of British University Libraries: An American Reaction." *International Library Review* 2 (1970): 135–173.

Library Trends 3:4 (Apr. 1955). "Current Acquisitions Trends in American Libraries." Robert Vosper, Issue Editor.

——— 12:4 (Apr. 1964). "European University Libraries: Current Status and Developments." Robert Vosper, Issue Editor.

——— 15:2 (Oct. 1966). "Current Trends in Collection Development in University Libraries." Jerrold Orne, Issue Editor.

——— 18:3 (Jan. 1970). "Problems of Acquisition for Research Libraries." Rolland E. Stevens, Issue Editor.

Liebaers, Herman. "Shared Cataloguing." *Unesco Bulletin for Libraries* 24 (1970): 62–72, 126–138.

Munby, A. N. L. and Lawrence W. Towner. *The Flow of Books and Manuscripts.* Los Angeles: William Andrews Clark Memorial Library, 1969.

Oxford University. *Report of the Committee on University Libraries* (The Shackleton Report). Oxford, 1966.

Powell, Lawrence Clark. *Bookman's Progress; the Selected Writings.* Los Angeles: Ward Ritchie Press, 1968.

Vosper, Robert. "Book Collecting for Libraries—the Greatest Game of All." *Bulletin of the Louisiana Library Association* 18 (1955): 73–81.

——— *The Farmington Plan Survey; A Summary of the Separate Studies of 1957–1961.* Urbana: Univ. of Illinois, 1965.

——— "International Implications of the Shared Cataloging Program: Planning for Resource Development." *Libri* 17 (1967): 285–293.

——— "There is No End." *College and Research Libraries* 20 (1959): 369–381.

Williams, Edwin E. *Farmington Plan Handbook.* Bloomington, Ind.: Association of Research Libraries, 1953. Rev. ed., 1961.

Wright, Louis B. and Gardon N. Ray. *The Private Collector and the Support of Scholarship.* Los Angeles: William Clark Memorial Library, 1969.

About the Author

Robert Vosper is universally regarded as one of the great bookmen in the profession today. Like Downs, he has devoted a large share of his strength to building up at UCLA's library the kind of magnificence in collections achieved by only a few academic libraries in our country. His earlier years in acquisitions at UCLA prepared him well for directing the University of Kansas Library in its rapid emergence as an important collection. When he returned to UCLA, the results were fairly predictable. In a very short time, that library has taken its place among the great collections in universities. He followed Downs' pattern in other ways—Chairman of the Farmington Plan Committee, President of ALA, Chairman of ARL, international service, and consultant to many government agencies. It is quite appropriate that out of this ample range of competence, we should ask Vosper to write about what he undoubtedly loves best—the acquiring of books.

LIBRARY EDUCATION

by Jack Dalton

When one recalls the observation that "any two philosophers can tell each other all they know in two hours,"[1] and when one reflects upon the substantial contributions to the making and recording of the history of education for librarianship in this country associated with the name of the man this volume honors, one may well wonder what I might have to say that has not been better said already. This will be particularly true for those who have happened upon a recent article in which I said all I want to say about current problems and trends in education for librarianship in the United States.[2] Under these circumstances, perhaps I may be permitted some reflections on the subject, a few questions for which I have not been able to find adequate answers, and the hope that I may be able to tease the reader into some speculation on his own or provoke him to respond with answers that have escaped me.

When Marianne Moore was asked on one occasion about her extensive use of quotations in her poems, she said, "I was just trying to be honorable and not to steal things. I've always felt that if a thing had been said in the *best* way, how can you say it better? If I wanted to say something and somebody had said it ideally, then I'd take it but give the person credit for it. That's all there is to it. If you are charmed by an author, I think it's a very strange and invalid imagination that doesn't long to share it. Somebody else should read it, don't you think?"[3] I agree. And since most of what I want to say has been thought about and written about and discussed by others, and since for about thirty years now I have been reading what my friends and their friends have been writing about professional education of all kinds—bibliothecal, medical, legal, graduate, and other, and since a good part of what they have suggested has gone unheeded, or so it seems to me, perhaps it will not be amiss to invite others to review a few of the things that have struck me. I shall quote freely.

Writing in *Library Notes* during the first months of the Columbia Library School, Melvil Dui let it be known that "the School prefers a small class carefully selected from a large number of those promising to do the best work in the profession."[4] He said, "There is already an overstock of mediocre librarians, assistants, and catalogers, and the influence of the school is intended to diminish rather than to increase their number." This was in 1887!* From his day to ours there has been a strong demand from many quarters for the schools to multiply those very numbers that Dui wanted to diminish. He was appropriately castigated in his day for much that he was supposed to have thought about librarianship and he has been attacked by some who hold that he wrecked a scholarly profession by setting up a trade school and setting our sights at the low level of library economy. It is instructive to muse upon what he and the other Dewey really had in mind and what their disciples made of their doctrines. Time and place make all the difference and the times made what they probably had to of Dui's ideas, but we should not overlook his stated intentions.

Thirty-five years later, when C. C. Williamson loosed some blasts of his own at library education, he said that while a librarian must, of course, understand library methods, "No amount of training in library technique can make a successful librarian of a person who lacks a good general education. The most essential part of training for librarianship is the general education that is ordinarily secured nowadays through a college course. . . . The time required for the specific training for librarianship is comparatively short . . . because the most important part of the equipment is general education and a knowledge of men and

* It is interesting to compare his view of the needs for a library school at that time with those expressed a few years later by Sir William Osler when he put forward a proposal for a school of librarianship at Oxford. He, too, had some things to say about the low level of activity which characterized the work and educational background of most of the practitioners of his time. His notes in 1907 and his address on the same subject before the Library Association ten years later are discussed by Harvey Cushing in *The Life of Sir William Osler*, Oxford, Clarendon Press, 1925, Vol. 2, pp. 81–82 and 573–574.

books which can be acquired in a variety of ways but which is most likely to be found in those who have completed a college degree."[5] The 1951 ALA *Standards of Accreditation* recognize this principle explicitly. Nowhere in that document is any program spoken of or referred to in terms other than a five-year program. The ALA policy statement on library education and manpower, adopted in 1970, says that "A good liberal education plus graduate-level study in the field of specialization (either in librarianship or in a relevant field) are seen as the minimum preparation for the kinds of assignments implied" for the first professional category.

In spite of our official agreement on this matter, and it is not necessary to repeat the arguments here, it is not always easy to make the point with admissions officers, deans, administrators or, for that matter, many members of faculties and librarians. They see no reason why one should not place the technical component of our educational programs in the undergraduate years and, some would argue, fairly far down within the undergraduate program, and certify librarians at a lower level. "Do you mean to say this man can't pass your courses?" one is asked upon refusing admission to a fine upstanding citizen who has compiled a brilliant record for two or three years at a decent college. Of course he can. I have known visiting foreign students holding only the Cambridge School Leaving Certificate to do quite well on all the basic courses, and we have all, I suspect, regretted at times that we did not feel justified in awarding a degree to such a student. Of course it isn't necessary to have a college degree to pass basic professional courses in any field. That is not the point, and this is not the place for a discussion of the history of our degree or the degradation of degrees in our time. It is enough to recall the recent efforts of all professional groups to upgrade the quality of their members. We all remember the relatively recent period when law schools and medical schools required only two years of college work for admission and the period of the "combined degree," when these schools tempted applicants, or tried to, into taking a third year of work at the undergraduate level, with the promise of a degree at the end of the first year of medical school or law school. Then there were increased requirements and, finally, the gradual general acceptance of the desirability of completing a liberal arts degree before beginning professional work.

Once again, these are matters that relate to time and place, and what is highly desirable for one country at one time may be impossible for another. I well recall a meeting in Rome in 1964 when a number of American librarians met with an equal number of librarians from the USSR to discuss matters of mutual interest. I was explaining our normal pattern of education in terms of years—twelve years of primary and secondary school, four years of college, *then* library school—when Mr. Konikov, then Director of the Lenin State Library, exploded with, "But isn't this frightfully expensive!" Of course it is, and few countries can afford it or have set it up this way.

It is worth adding here that more than one library school recognized the need of upgrading its program before other units within its own institution felt the need. Williamson pointed out, for example, in his first annual report at Columbia (1926) that the School of Library Service was that institution's "only professional school on a strictly graduate basis."[6] This is not the place to consider the confusion and misunderstanding, not to say nonsense, that have engulfed much educational writing dealing with such terms as "graduate," "professional," "graduate-professional," and the like.

As all nations have come to rely more and more upon professionally trained men and women, and as the demand for the services of people so trained has increased, institutions of higher learning have generally recognized their increased responsibility for the men and women trained in their professional schools. One of the things that first attracted me to Columbia University was the recognition of this responsibility and its stated policy toward professional training within a university. A 1956 outline of plans for its future discusses the implications of university status for professional schools and states the conviction that the "quality of a program of professional education must be measured by the use it makes of the intellectual resources of the university as well as the contribution it renders to other parts of the university community."[7] This notion is worth pondering. In my conversations with my colleagues, in my discussions with students, and in my visits—formal and informal—to many library schools, I have yet to encounter an instance in which it seemed to me that the library school was making adequate use of the intellectual resources of the parent institution or making a very serious effort to increase its own contribution.*

*Unhappily, I do not believe that the library schools are alone in this. If I were a university president with an extra life to spare, I would like to spend it on this problem.

The same Columbia statement sets forth so clearly my own view on one other important topic that I used it for several years as a frontispiece to the bulletin of the School of Library Service. It reads:

> . . . no program of professional education terminating in the first professional degree should be designed to train individuals for narrow specialties within a given profession. Such a curriculum gives the student what he can, in all probability, learn on the job, and thus neglects the obligation to give him what he is unlikely to get elsewhere. Further, it neglects the importance of providing knowledge and skills that are broad enough in character to allow the prospective professional man or woman to move easily from one position to another, including posts of general responsibility within the profession. Finally, a narrowly based curriculum overlooks the fact that professional activity requires not simply the mastery of a specialized body of knowledge or of certain technical performances, but also the selective application of such knowledge and skills to complicated human problems. It is not only expertness that is required, but also such qualities as insight, imagination, sensitivity, and ethical responsibility.[8]

When one considers the many things library schools are asked to do these days, the objections to what they are doing, the frequently voiced demand that they change their programs to produce the kind of person one might reasonably expect from a cross between a good teachers' college and school of social work, one wonders about the very concepts "library" and "librarian" and thinks wistfully of that genius who once remarked "a definition a day keeps the charlatans away." Library schools must certainly *share* the burden of clarification, but the job is not theirs alone. It *is* the job of each school to make as clear as it can with words and deeds what *it* is trying to do, what it believes to be the most important next-steps and long-range goals, and how it proposes to attain them.

I recently attended a two-day conference which brought together a knowledgeable group of library users who began their deliberations with a series of good questions, the first two of which were: "What is the role of the public library today?" and "How can the public library play a greater role?" At the end of two days they were stuck in a thicket of questions which would have been self-answering if answers to the original two had been agreed upon. Our failure to reach agreement on such basic matters, even for purposes of discussion, dooms us to countless profitless hours. Perhaps the most important job for the library schools these next few years is not teaching students but defining roles and goals. This problem of knowing ourselves has been neglected for so long that Eli Ginzberg, in a study that has not received the attention it deserves, was moved to conclude:

> Our final finding and recommendation is that the field of librarianship broaden and deepen its knowledge of itself. There are too few facts and the facts that are available are frequently of such questionable quality that a responsible leadership cannot formulate action programs and press for solutions. If the leaders are to lead and not be pushed by events they must devote more time and energy to encouraging systematic research into their profession. Only with sound knowledge of the past and the present, will it be possible to formulate plans for the future.[9]

In formulating these plans, how should one think about the librarian? What manner of man is he?

More than thirty-five years ago, José Ortega y Gasset asked, "Is it too Utopian to imagine in a not too distant future librarians held responsible by society for the regulation of the production of books, in order to avoid the publication of superfluous ones and, on the other hand, to guard against the lack of those demanded by the complex of vital problems in every age?"[10] He concluded his essay with the suggestion that "The mission of the librarian ought to be, not as it is today the simple administration of the things called books, but the adjustment, the setting to rights, of that vital function which is the book."[11] This is precisely the kind of problem Jacques Barzun had in mind when, speaking of the new librarian he believed society needed, he asked "What kind of professional is the librarian?"[12] He is convinced that "the knowledge explosion is a myth. . . . The avalanche of paper is real enough, and there may indeed be an increase in the quantity of recorded facts . . . Barely an increase in information."[13] And then, "If this conclusion is correct, it has numerous grave implications, of which I believe the most momentous is the responsibility it puts upon the librarian. Only the librarian can save us from perishing under the suffocating materials shot from the ceaseless Vesuvius. . . . In the end the New Librarian must be the chooser of books and pruner of collections . . . the man of reading and judgment who won recognition and compensation by performing the rarest service next to lifesaving, namely, the exact and expert communication of intelligence."[14] *

They deserve repeating, those phrases: "that vital function which is the book" and "the exact and expert communication of intelligence."

If I may extend this a little further, let me invite you to hold these notions of the librarian's job in mind while glancing at a stimulating article by P. B. Medawar,[15] the 1960 Nobel Prize winner in medicine and Director of the National Institute for Medical Research. Concerned with popular misconceptions of the scientific process of thought and the ignorance and utter confusion that exist in the layman's mind, Medawar opens his discussion with this paragraph:

> Science is essentially a growth of organised factual knowledge . . . and as science advances, the burden of factual information which it adds to daily is becoming well nigh insupportable. A time will surely come when the scientist must train not for the traditional three or four years, but for ten or more, if he is to equip himself as a front-line combatant in the battle for knowledge. As things are, the scientist avoids being crushed beneath this factual burden by taking refuge in specialisation, and the increase of specialisation is the distinguishing mark of modern scientific growth. Because of it, scientists are becoming progressively less well able to communicate with each other, let alone with the outside world; and we must look forward to an ever finer fragmentation of knowledge, in which each specialist will live in a tiny world of his own. St. Thomas Aquinas was the last. . . .[16]

And then he asks and answers:

> True or false, all this?—False, I should say, in every particular. The idea that Science is essentially a classified inventory of factual information is of the same intellectual stature as that which treats History as a chronology of dates. . . . The ballast of factual information, so far from being just about to sink us, is growing daily less. The factual burden of a science varies inversely with its degree of maturity. As a science advances, particular facts are comprehended

---

* It is instructive to compare the Ortega and Barzun essays at many points. It is also instructive to compare the librarian's job as Barzun outlines it with the job of librarian as seen by the various writers on the library college idea. I have felt at times that the latter fail to distinguish between what have been called "acquiry" and "inquiry" in the educational process and I think the failure to make this distinction leads to much fruitless discussion and confusion.

within, and therefore in a sense annihilated by, general statements of steadily increasing explanatory power and compass—whereupon the facts are forgotten, for they have no further right to independent existence. Biology before Darwin was almost all facts . . . but biology is over the hump . . . and physics is far enough advanced that an eminent physicist recently told me, with the air of one not wishing to be overheard, that the science itself was drawing to a close. . . .[17]

These points need not be labored, but they should be kept in mind as one observes sadly how many of our programs are cluttered with more and more courses covering every trivial detail of operation—how few the general statements and how great their insistence upon the need for ever longer programs. We do not need longer programs; we desperately need better programs, more clearly defined programs, and a clearer understanding of the profession to which we attempt to introduce students through our basic programs.

What are those basic programs today? They change slowly, but by and large they consist, with here and there some sort of concession to what is variously called information science or documentation or computer technology or data processing or something of the sort, of a group of courses that cover in an introductory fashion technical services, reference and bibliography, some type of orientation course (generally much disliked by all hands), literature courses and usually a brief introduction to administrative problems. All too frequently, some of these are relegated to the undergraduate years, and sometimes it seems as if it does not matter which years. It is hard to tell from examining many program statements whether this core does not matter or whether all that follows is a matter of little consequence. There has been a good deal of discussion through the years of the poor old core, but it is time that another serious attack upon it was launched. Unhappily, the profession has not been able to make up its mind what constitutes the basic preparation for librarianship. The bulletin of the graduate school of business that I know best describes its core courses in this way:

> Core materials provide an understanding of the general environment and operations of business. These materials have been developed to stimulate a man to become a student of business throughout his career, regardless of the field of his assignment or the functional nature of his successive tasks.[18]

Not a bad starting point for our discussions. Whatever we claim for our core, it is hardly so much; whatever we attempt, it should be at least this much.

In 1959 there were thirty ALA-accredited library schools in the United States and Canada and many people thought this number too small; today we have almost twice that number and others waiting in line, and many people think this number too large. ALA now has two subcommittees of its Committee on Accreditation working on standards for undergraduate and graduate programs of education. These committees work in the knowledge that today there are almost unbelievable differences among the schools—differences in admissions requirements, expectations, programs, conceptions, and vision. In spite of much discussion of the stultifying effect of standards on professional education, I believe ours have allowed for enough flexibility to permit any reasonable experiment yet introduced or seriously discussed. In 1970, ALA adopted a new policy statement that could, given a strong committee on accreditation, have a far-reaching effect on librarianship; one hopes the committee will recognize its opportunity.

Our one international fraternity in librarianship has as its motto "Scholarship and Service." We have always been long on the one and short on the other. We have never had, and we do not have today, our share of young scholars and the need for sound scholarship has never been greater. Of course, we want people imbued with ideals of service—this goes without saying in a professional school indeed, it is one of the elements of the definition of a profession, but the schools must be dedicated to the discipline and a rigorous demonstration of the full majesty and demands of that discipline. The schools must give the student that conception, and understanding of their profession that Archibald Mac-Leish had in mind for another profession when he said on one occasion of Mr. Justice Holmes, "What he gave them . . . was an understanding of the relation of the law to life which made impossible a conception of the law as anything but a means to an end. To most great lawyers the law sooner or later becomes a substantive—a noun. To Mr. Justice Holmes it was always a verb having a predicate to follow."[19] That is the conception of librarianship needed to help overcome the difficulty of what Felix Frankfurter has called "a rigid outlook upon a dynamic world."[20] And we could all ponder profitably and apply to our own investigations these musings by Holmes: "I look forward to a time when the part played by history in the explanation of dogma shall be very small and instead of ingenious research we shall spend our energy on a study of the ends sought to be attained and the reasons for desiring them."[21]

"The Ends Sought to be Attained and the Reasons for Desiring Them"

This is the study with which the schools should be eternally occupied. But what are some of the things with which they are most likely to be concerned in the years immediately ahead? Is there any likelihood that there will be large areas of agreement among them? Unhappily, I fear not. A few years ago there was some discussion of the possibility of bringing together the eight or ten library schools in the New York–Massachusetts–Pennsylvania area for a recruiting evening. The idea was that we would take over the Grand Ballroom of the Waldorf for the evening, invite to dinner all the student counselors and advisers in the area—high school and college—and make a general presentation of what was required, what was needed, what was acceptable. The discussion did not get very far. The diversity among them was too great. We are not yet together on such simple matters as admission requirements, whether foreign language study is an absolute necessity or a waste of time, and whether any college degree is adequate evidence of the fitness of a candidate for librarianship or whether there are certain desirable and necessary minimum qualifications. Many of us require some form of testing, usually the aptitude tests of the Graduate Record Examination. The Educational Testing Service, which prepares this examination, has prepared the Law School Aptitude Test for the law schools of the country. I am told by my colleagues in the law schools that it is a good test and tells them much of what they want to know about a student's aptitude for legal study. Imagine for a moment the kinds of questions that would arise in our present state of ignorance of ourselves if we tried to reach agreement on such a test!

Why is this so? "No school has attempted or is now prepared to disregard what has been done in the past and make a thorough, scientific analysis of what training for professional library work should be and build its curriculum upon its finding, instead of following tradition and imitating others."[22] Williamson said this fifty years ago; it is still true. When he had an opportunity shortly thereafter to see what one man could do he probably had more than one occasion to reflect upon these musings of Tolstoi:

> The activity of a commander-in-chief does not at all resemble the activity we imagine to ourselves when we sit at ease in our studies examining some campaign on the map, with a certain number of troops on this and that side in a certain known locality, and begin our plans from some given moment. A commander-in-chief is never dealing with the beginning of any event—the position from which we always contemplate it. The commander-in-chief is always in the midst of a series of shifting events and so he never can at any moment consider the whole import of an event that is occurring. Moment by moment the event is imperceptibly shaping itself, and at every moment of this continuous, uninterrupted shaping of events the commander-in-chief is in the midst of a most complex play of intrigues, worries, contingencies, authorities, projects, counsels, threats and deceptions, and is continually obliged to reply to innumerable questions addressed to him, which constantly conflict with one another.[23]

One of the people who has been able to start a library school pretty much from scratch is Andrew Osborn. To those who have not seen it, I commend Number 2 of the *Library and Information Studies* issued by the School of Library and Information Science of the University of Western Ontario, and entitled "Two Parallel Disciplines: Education and Library and Information Science." This little brochure is his skillful paraphrase of the 1966 *Report of the Harvard Committee on the Graduate Study of Education.*

> The purpose of this report is to consider how the graduate study of librarianship should properly be conceived in the setting of a strong independent university . . . the question was asked how the university should ideally conceive its responsibilities for the study of library and information science in the world as it now is and as it promises to be. This fundamental question has led us into numerous and complexly linked issues.
> What is the proper scope of the study of librarianship, and how may it be structured within the university? What, in general, is the suitable role of professional study within a university setting? How are the demands of scholarship, research, professional training and service to be adjusted to one another? What principles of integration

may facilitate such mutual adjustment? Is there a fundamental science of librarianship, or a unifying set of fundamental studies, or perhaps some form of common training experience or other device that may lend coherence to the various demands of library studies?

How should such study, furthermore, be oriented to the world outside the university? Should it, for example, be organized so as to follow the lead of professional practice and the existing structure of professional roles, or should it set itself the task of revising practice and restructuring roles? What, further, should be its relation to social problems arising within the sphere of professional concern? Can it calmly disregard them without threat to its integrity and keep its attention focused on abstract questions above the battle? Conversely, can it find realistic ways to express engagement in social issues without compromising either its scholarly standards or professional authority?

Aside from the scope of library studies and their relations to university, profession, and society, there are related problems that concern rather its internal organization and its execution. How, for example, should such studies be divided for the purposes of instruction and research, and how may the isolating effects latent in any such division be overcome? What should degrees in library and information science represent, and how should programs leading to such degrees be conceived? How may clinical practice, internship, and supervision be fruitfully joined with scholarly and research training? How is research itself to be developed and organized in a field where the social impact of research is relatively direct and of far-reaching significance? What sorts of professional roles should be envisaged as accessible to graduates of library science programs? How may recruitment of ablest students be improved? How should the roles of faculty members be conceived, and how may their duties be most fruitfully allocated.[24]

I have quoted from the brochure at length because these lines seem to me to bring together so many of the questions with which those of us who have worked in library schools have in recent years struggled, and perhaps because even though I do not feel envious myself, I understand those who do envy the man who can start his considerations with a clean slate. If I may be permitted a little paraphrasing of my own, I might say that "the life of a library school, as most of us find them, as of an individual, is a palimpsest. What has been, or at least what we think about what has been, may very considerably influence what will be. The shape of things to come depends not a little upon the remembrance of things past."[25]

Our chief problem is the complex and eternally challenging problem of all professional schools, namely, the problem of relating properly the sources from which we draw our strength, the work of the school, and the requirements of the profession. To forget our need of that deep and continuing study and understanding of the materials with which we deal would be as disastrous as it would be for a law school to try to operate without political scientists, or medical schools without biologists, or business schools without economists, or engineering schools without mathematicians and physicists. On the other hand, to overlook the needs of the profession we serve and to become too much removed from direct contact with it is to deserve the criticism one frequently hears. A perilous balance, to be sure, but one that must be maintained. I believe that our biggest problem for some time to come is likely to be that of recruiting in considerable numbers from supporting disciplines young scholars who are willing to devote themselves to the strictly bibliothecal aspects of their fields. I need not point out here what has been pointed out so eloquently by Weinberg and others of the opportunities and satisfactions that await them.

Daniel Bell, the social scientist I most enjoy reading and the author of the most provocative work on general education that I have encountered,[26] has been a guiding spirit in the American Academy of Arts and Sciences Commission on the Year 2000. He concludes his essay "The Trajectory of an Idea" with some observations on serendipity and synergism, of which you have probably heard too much in recent years, and then with these wise words: "Yet serendipity and synergism are examples of that which is unpremeditated and unpredictable. This is a paradox and a chastening one for a group that seeks earnestly to anticipate, if not to predict, the future."[27]

One can easily forecast the hundred technical innovations likely to be made during the years ahead. One can assume the capabilities that will permit instant transfer of stored information in usable form over any distance. But when INTREX and IMPRESS and all the experiments and research that such acronyms suggest have been completed and have brought us to the time when all information available at any given moment is recorded in the most convenient form and is instantly available to the outermost library outpost, and when there is a console on the desk of every student who wishes one, from kindergarten to retired scholar, and when all data systems are compatible, and when every librarian is fully "aware," what then is the librarian's role? Is that the end to be attained? Or just the beginning?

I used to worry, as dean, about what seemed to me to be a willingness and a readiness on the part of some schools and some educators to swap keyboards. We had not erased completely from our catalogs the old requirement, which disturbed a lot of people, that every student be able to type, before we were preoccupied with another kind of keyboard operation. I am not complaining about the advent of the computer. Far from it. I want to see libraries completely computerized as rapidly as possible. I think it probable that the social impact of the computer has as yet been only dimly perceived. I am concerned about a tendency to assume that, even at its highest capacity, the computer can ever be anything more than an aid to the kind of librarian Ortega and Barzun were talking about and the kind our schools should have in mind in their planning. And I am concerned about the apparent willingness of some schools to devote themselves to training at low levels, for a computerized civilization, a group who will simply move into the seats left vacant by those assistants at typewriters operating at the low level Dui was talking about—the group many of us have hoped the computer would help us eliminate from our libraries.

If Ortega and Barzun were asking for more than society is willing to allow, then whose problem is it? And until that time comes when, from somewhere, there appears a new breed to assume the role they had in mind—a role that can easily be linked to the role Weinberg must have been thinking about when he made his plea to the scientific community to devote more of their talent to the information problem—are the librarians simply to be the caretakers? Not good enough. Is it too much to ask that they consider the suggested role? When one thinks about the problems of individual values, and privacy, and freedom, and how the bureaucracy with the greatest control over the information will affect the lives of all of us, is it not clear that the central role which the librarian must play in the information story demands more than the educational hodgepodge of unplanned courses at the undergraduate level and free electives at the fifth-year level which we have heretofore found acceptable? Is the title "Librarian" to be conferred upon any man or woman of good will regardless of intellectual attainments? Of course one wants both; the schools must require both. But in the years ahead our society will not entrust to the kindest of people the jobs that must be done, unless these same people are also hard-headed, intelligent, critical, and wise. The schools are in a position to make certain demands and state certain conditions and the time is right for them to move. It will be a pity if they do not, but no one is going to press them hard. Their history does not suggest that they are revolutionaries. Unfortunately, it is going to take a revolution to bring about the necessary changes. Nothing else will suffice and nothing the profession has ever done approaches in importance the need for the critical self-examination I have in mind. If we could bring it off, we would provide an exercise in intellectual devotion which would present our colleagues in other professional schools in the universities with a sorely needed example, apprise them of the true nature of librarianship, and—who knows—perhaps even awaken them to their own desperate condition.

References

1. Charles P. Curtis, Jr., and Ferris Greenslet, eds., *The Practical Cogitator* (Boston: Houghton Mifflin Co., 1945), p. 3.
2. I have in mind particularly Robert Downs' fine summary account of "Education for Librarianship in the United States and Canada," which appeared in Larry Earl Bone, ed., *Library Education: An International Survey* (Champaign, Illinois: University of Illinois Graduate School of Library Science, 1968), pp. 1–20. My own paper appeared as "Library Education and Research in Librarianship, Some Current Problems and Trends in the United States," *Libri* XXI:3 (1969): 157–174.
3. An interview with Donald Hall in *The Paris Review*, Winter, 1961, issue; reprinted in *A Marianne Moore Reader* (New York: Viking Press, 1965), p. 260.
4. As reprinted in *School of Library Economy of Columbia College, 1887–1889— Documents for a History* (New York: Columbia University, School of Library Service, 1937), p. 112.
5. Charles C. Williamson, *Training for Library Service* (New York: Carnegie Corporation, 1923), p. 6.
6. Ray Trautman, *A History of the School of Library Service, Columbia University* (New York: Columbia University Press, 1954), p. 47.
7. *Report of the President's Committee on the Educational Future of Columbia University* (New York: Columbia University, 1957), p. 12.
8. Ibid.
9. Eli Ginzberg and Carol A. Brown, *Manpower for Library Services* (New York: Columbia University, Conservation of Human Resources Project, 1967), p. 44.
10. José Ortega y Gasset, *The Mission of the Librarian* (Boston: G. K. Hall & Co., 1961), p. 21. In the translation by James Lewis and Ray Carpenter.

11. Ibid., p. 22.
12. Jacques Barzun, "The New Librarian to the Rescue," *Library Journal* (Nov. 1, 1969): 3963.
13. Ibid., p. 3964.
14. Ibid., p. 3965.
15. P. B. Medawar, "Anglo-Saxon Attitudes," *Encounter* (Aug. 1965): 52–58.
16. Ibid., p. 52.
17. Ibid.
18. Bulletin of the Graduate School of Business of Columbia University for 1970–1971, p. 31.
19. Archibald MacLeish and E. F. Prichard, Jr., eds., *Law and Politics, Occasional Papers of Felix Frankfurter, 1913–1938* (New York: Capricorn Books, 1962), p. xviii.
20. Ibid., p. 348.
21. Ibid., p. xxi.
22. Williamson, op. cit, p. 25.
23. Tolstoi, *War and Peace,* Vol. II (New York: Heritage Press, 1938), pp. 308–309.
24. "Two Parallel Disciplines: Education and Library and Information Science," *Library and Information Studies* (University of Western Ontario, 1967), no. 2, pp. 3–4.
25. MacLeish and Prichard, op. cit., p. 346.
26. Daniel Bell, *The Reforming of General Education* (New York: Columbia University Press, 1966).
27. Daniel Bell, "The Year 2000—The Trajectory of an Idea," *Daedalus* (Summer, 1967): 651.

About the Author

Teacher, librarian, former dean of Columbia School of Library Service, ALA executive, and southern gentleman, Jack Dalton has all of these attributes in common with Bob Downs. Jack came out of Virginia and Bob from North Carolina; their working contacts were frequent in each of these fields for more than thirty years. The field of education for librarianship was a natural for both of them, and Dalton's reflections based on his long experience at Columbia could undoubtedly be matched, line for line, by Downs.

LIBRARY SURVEYS

by Stephen A. McCarthy and Murray L. Howder

The literature of librarianship is not as extensive as that of many other fields. There are landmark books and classics, but there is nothing like the proliferation of publications in the library field that there is even in some of the subfields of education. This may be a cause for rejoicing or for regret, depending on one's point of view.

What is true of librarianship in general is also true of the university library field. Instead of a substantial group of books covering the field as a whole or developing certain aspects in detail, the number of full-length works is small and shows little or no sign of increasing significantly. Speculation on the reasons for this situation could take several directions, and perhaps a plausible rationale could be developed to support whatever explanation appealed to the writer.

Our present purpose is more modest. It is to consider a part of the output of one university librarian, to make an appraisal of it, and in the process to note some reflections on these professional contributions. As earlier essays have shown, Bob Downs has been far more of a writing librarian than many of his colleagues. But even a cursory review of his bibliography reveals that a substantial part of his writing has consisted of studies, surveys, and reports based on visits, inspections, conferences, and inquiries.

This points to something of interest and importance about the literature and the subliterature of university librarianship. Though the formal works in the field may be relatively few in number, the more informal report and survey literature is abundant. This literature has flourished and apparently continues to do so, yet it is not nearly as well known and recognized as it should be. By comparison, the report literature of science and technology is well organized, recorded, and available for distribution.

Library surveys and reports are in many cases ad hoc. They result from efforts to appraise a situation and recommend improvements. Much of the task may be accomplished in conferences and discussions, which the report distills and reiterates. The report is in a sense a by-product. Frequently, such reports are never published; they may or may not get into the bibliographic record and they are not available on the market. Instead, they are frequently "issued" by the subject library, and copies may be obtained from the author or from the institution. Thus the report literature in the field of university librarianship, which may best represent the current thinking of professionally active university librarians, may go largely unnoticed by colleagues and fellow librarians. There is, however, some reason to believe that much of this material is made available to library schools, and thus it may be more effectively brought to the attention of students than might be supposed. It is a significant part of the record of university libraries describing their activities, problems, and efforts to solve them over the past half century. As such, it would seem to merit more attention than is commonly accorded to it.

As one of the most active and literate university librarians of our time, Downs has naturally made many contributions to library survey literature. His work spans a generation and appropriately began with a study of research materials in his native state of North Carolina in 1937. From that date to 1969, he has produced at least fifty studies, surveys and reports, both published and unpublished. From North Carolina he has moved across the continent and north to Canada, south to Mexico and Latin America, west to Japan, and east to Turkey. En route he stopped at Slippery Rock!

The breadth of Downs' subject interests matched his geographic range, extending from resources to site locations, from union catalogs and technical services to personnel procedures and library education. Intensive studies of specific problems in a single library and assessments of the libraries of a state, region, or country, as well as the more common general survey of a university library system, are all part of the Downs record. His emphasis on resources, a term generally used to mean collections or holdings, was evident in some of his earliest work and it has continued to receive substantial attention in many of his studies. The same term, "resources," is used with a much broader connotation in several of his studies of groups of libraries in a state or region.

Since it is neither feasible nor desirable to attempt to review a series of studies individually, a somewhat arbitrary grouping of the major studies into categories has been made. In characterizing the several groups, individual studies will be used as examples and illustrations of the methods employed in attacking the problems and presenting the findings.

HOLDINGS OR RESOURCES SURVEYS

Downs' first effort in this field resulted from his chairmanship of a Committee on the Resources of Southern Libraries. He used the descriptive essay to characterize and evaluate research collections, emphasizing the weakness of southern research collections by comparing them with collections in other regions. Both of these approaches, and especially the descriptive essay as a means of reporting library holdings, tend to reappear in later studies.

The purpose of this study of the research collections in thirteen southern states was to call attention to needs and to stimulate interest and support in correcting them. It noted that in many instances "strong" academic departments were not well supported by strong book and periodical collections and that there were far too many "southern collections." The lack of comprehensive collections of newspapers and government publications was noted with the recommendation that a coordinated policy for the development of such collections was needed. Existing cooperative programs were regarded as significant, but more cooperative efforts were required. Recommendations included contributions from these southern libraries to the National Union Catalog, a union list of periodicals, a thorough survey of resources for research and a special project for the strengthening of bibliographic resources.

Downs' two major works dealing with holdings or resources developed from his study of southern libraries. The first, using the same title as his committee report, is *Resources of Southern Libraries; a Survey of Facilities for Research,* published by the ALA in 1938. In this work, the research collections of 316 libraries in thirteen southern states are described in essay form. The book is organized into chapters under broad subject areas with the principal collections presented in order of size and importance. A detailed subject index facilitates checking the text for references to specific topics. Except for illustrative titles of major works and sets, or rare and unusual titles, the method employed does not afford precise information on the location of a given title.

This inability to obtain assured location information, and, to a lesser extent, detailed bibliographic data, is sometimes considered to lessen the value of such survey works and to emphasize instead the usefulness of union catalogs. The purposes of the two types of publications— descriptive essays and union catalogs—are different, and each is of value for its particular function. The bibliographic essay is, first of all, intended to be readable, to be factually correct and to convey to the reader a summary view of the extent, depth, and nature of the collections being described. The union catalog, on the other hand, emphasizes information, location, and completeness. There may be readers of union catalogs, but they are few in number. Instead, union catalogs are consulted for the precise factual information they contain. The bibliographic essay can only be written after examining what might be called an "ad hoc union catalog," or a series of individual catalogs; whereas an examination of a union catalog, if any lasting impression is to be retained, requires the examiner to produce and remember his own bibliographic essay or summary.

Production of the bibliographic essay, if well done, is not a simple and easy task, but it is still far less laborious than the compilation of a union catalog. For this reason, it is also less expensive and thus more feasible. The bibliographic essay is commonly based on a combination of questionnaires and personal visits, as was the case in *Resources of Southern Libraries.*

Downs' second book of this type, *Resources of New York City Libraries; a Survey of Facilities for Advanced Study and Research,* describes and evaluates research collections of over 400 libraries in the greater New York area. The plan of the work is similar to *Southern Libraries* and it is intended to serve the same purpose, that of a general guide to the library collections for research use in the metropolitan area.

Both of these works are worthy examples of the kind of publications they are intended to be. They are not designed to take the place of union catalogs; they have another objective and they attain it. More publications of this kind would be of value in guiding researchers, bibliographers, and librarians.

CATALOGS AND CATALOGING

Downs was responsible as editor and author for three publications in this area of librarianship. His first contribution was that of editor of the ALA publication, *Union Catalogs in the United States,* a collection of essays or papers on the subject. This book presents several concepts which came to prevail in subsequent years. It stresses the importance of the National Union Catalog and argues that it should have the highest priority. The need for careful planning in the development of regional catalogs is noted in order to ensure full coverage with a minimum of overlapping. The lack of financial stability on a continuing basis is recognized as a serious weakness of regional union catalogs, and the value of these catalogs is perceived as a function of their proximity to Washington. Subsequent experience has borne out the validity of these observations.

Downs' second publication, primarily in the field of cataloging, was his report on the National Diet Library. Although not solely devoted to cataloging and classification, this section of the report is the most significant part. Downs followed Charles H. Brown and Verner W. Clapp by six months on a mission to Japan, in accordance with recommendations made by the first visitors. It was Downs' assignment to outline the steps to be taken to get the collection of the National Diet Library classified and cataloged and, through this operation, to establish centralized processing for government libraries. In addition, a card service similar to that of the Library of Congress was to be established. This service, it was expected, would be a strong force working toward general acceptance by Japanese libraries of the classification and subject heading systems adopted by the Diet Library. Downs' recommendations here are clear and forthright but at the same time perceptive of the nuances of the Japanese situation. As opportunity has offered in the ensuing years, the Diet Library has moved to implement the recommended programs.

In the summer of 1949, Downs served briefly as the Acting Chief of the Union Catalog Division of the Library of Congress. This appointment was intended to secure the benefit of an informed outside view on the problems of the Union Catalog and guidance to its future development. Many of Downs' recommendations have come to pass in the twenty years that have elapsed since his report was written. Selected libraries are now reporting their acquisitions regularly to the Union Catalog, and the holdings reported by those libraries are included in the published *National Union Catalog*. The problem of subject access is met by the subject section of the catalog. The retrospective Union Catalog is in the process of publication; and the *Union Catalog of Manuscript Collections* has been published, with a plan for the issuance of supplements.

Several of Downs' recommendations have not been acted on. The regional union catalogs have not been added en bloc to the *National Union Catalog*. The Library of Congress has not established a national union catalog of serials nor has it taken action to provide or see to the provision of serial indexes or abstracts in fields not satisfactorily covered by existing indexes. There is now reason to hope that the three National Libraries will accept responsibility for developing and maintaining a national record of serials in machine readable form.

SURVEYS OF INDIVIDUAL UNIVERSITY LIBRARIES

The term "library survey" is most commonly used for the detailed study of an individual library. Downs has been responsible for four such studies at Utah, Georgia, Purdue, and Brigham Young, and he collaborated with Wilson and Tauber on the Cornell survey. His evaluation of Kabul University Library for AID should perhaps also be placed in this group. These reports tend to follow a pattern, with additions or omissions of some elements in recognition of specific local needs or problems. Thus, for example, he argues for the acceptance of federal funds at Brigham Young, and he examines the special problems of locating and using library materials under the divisional plan of organization as developed at Georgia.

The Purdue survey may be used as an example of this type of study. Purdue is seen as an institution in transition from a technical and scientific university to a broad, general university offering advanced degrees in all major fields of study. The advanced degree programs and the students enrolling in them have come in a relatively short time and the library collections to support them have not been developed on a commensurate scale. Substantial collection buildup is required. Review of the library support record makes it clear that significant and sustained attention to library requirements will be necessary. More effective administrative arrangements appear desirable to give the library greater strength in the university. A model statute based on the Illinois statute is proposed as a corrective. Similarly, a higher degree of centralization, but with some planned decentralization, is recommended. The building problem is regarded as central and the solution recommended is a new structure. Peculiarities and deficiencies in the acquisitions and cataloging operations of the libraries are noted and changes designed to simplify and expedite these functions are put forward. Downs' concern with the strength of the collections is manifested in a rather substantial review of holdings under categories roughly approximating academic departments. Personnel policies are reviewed with approval, but the serious need for a significantly larger staff is noted. The study concludes with an analysis of faculty and student responses to a questionnaire regarding library collections and services. The program set forth in the recommendations may well require ten years to accomplish.

SURVEY OF GROUPS OF LIBRARIES

Downs has also been responsible as author or editor for six studies of groups of libraries or, in several instances, for all or most of the libraries of a region or a state. His principal work of this kind has been in Arkansas, Missouri, and North Carolina. Both the Missouri and North Carolina studies represent a cooperative effort to assess the present state of library affairs in the respective states and to recommend the most seriously needed improvements. In these studies Downs served as a planner and director of the study and as editor and author of the reports. The detailed collections of data were carried out by committees of librarians working under Downs' direction.

Taking *Resources of North Carolina Libraries*, 1965, as the chief example of the state study, we find that the library services of the state are considered inadequate. Resources, facilities, and personnel are judged insufficient to meet needs. After evaluating all libraries from the state library to school and special libraries, the study recommends higher levels of funding, new and improved facilities, and training and recruitment programs to provide the personnel required.

RESOURCES OF CANADIAN ACADEMIC AND RESEARCH LIBRARIES

The Canadian survey is reserved for separate treatment because it is the most extensive study of this type in the Downs bibliography. The study was sponsored by the Association of Universities and Colleges of Canada, responding to a proposal originating with the Canadian Association of College and University Libraries. The principal lines of inquiry were determined by a steering committee chaired by Robert Blackburn and funding was supplied by the Canada Council and the Council on Library Resources. A survey staff of three Canadian librarians, with special assistance from others, undertook the main task of collecting the necessary data. In carrying out this assignment the staff visited every university library in Canada, as well as many college, public, government, and special libraries. The printed report running to 300 pages was published in both English and French.

The organization of the report on a study of this scope presents some problems, in that evaluations and recommendations must be made in somewhat generalized terms and they may thus be open to the charge of being no more than admonitions of perfection. In any case, the presentation used sets forth first a series of some forty recommendations, moves on to a brief review of related previous studies and reports, and then describes in profile form the universities and colleges of Canada.

Following this introductory chapter, the report consists of separate chapters on Administrative Organization; Technical Services; Readers' Services and Use; Physical Facilities; Personnel; Faculty and Student Views on Library Service; Library Automation and Mechanization; Library Cooperation and Interrelationships; Financial Support; Resources for Study and Research; and Some Specialized Collections in Canadian

Libraries. Interspersed throughout are some thirty tables reporting data on many aspects of the subjects under review.

Although the pattern of development varies, the approach used in many of the chapters is to introduce the principal topic with a general discussion followed by references to standards and observations regarding accepted good practice. Subsequently, the situation that he found in Canadian university libraries is set forth in tables or textually, as appropriate. Subtopics are noted briefly with comments that relate to the Canadian situation. Chapters close with a summary that emphasizes main points, encourages promising developments already underway, and points the way to desirable improvements.

The list of specialized collections with brief descriptive notes, although admittedly incomplete, provides a useful addendum. Similarly, the "Bibliographical References to Canadian Library Resources" helps to round out the study.

This study presents a broad, yet detailed, picture of Canadian university libraries in the mid-'60s. Given this assessment as a basis on which to build and with the recommendations throughout the report, as well as the special presentation of major points at the outset, the Canadian university library community is fully supplied with the information needed to increase, substantially, its strength and usefulness. The work to be done and the costs to be met are great. From a distance one can only hope that an adequate measure of each may be provided to our good neighbors.

Although the report notes the leadership role of the National Library and the National Science Library, it does not attempt to project the programs by which this leadership can be exercised for the benefit of the Canadian academic community. Developments of the past few years in Ottawa make it clear that if this report were being written in 1970, greater emphasis would undoubtedly be given to existing and potential programs of the national libraries.

UNPUBLISHED REPORTS

These reports, thirty in number, range from a few pages to one report of over a hundred pages. Most of them, however, are short and are devoted to specific subjects. Some of them are quick, brief surveys, others relate to library buildings and space, still others to library education and personnel. They are further evidence of the important professional contributions of R. B. Downs.

Taken as a whole, the surveys, studies, reports, and evaluations constitute a record of service and achievement in which the author should find much satisfaction.

LIBRARY SURVEYS AND THE FUTURE

In a recently published article, ["Three Early Academic Library Surveys," *College and Research Libraries* xxx (Nov. 1969): 498–505], Norman Stevens estimates that there have probably been some sixty full-scale academic library surveys in the past thirty-five years, only half of which have been recorded in *Library Literature*. This illustrates the problem. Some, perhaps many, surveys are little known beyond the subject institutions and the authors. Short of a questionnaire, it would not be possible to compile a list or make a count, and the results would hardly warrant the effort required.

Instead, we may safely say that the survey has proved to be a useful means of focusing attention on library problems in colleges and universities and has commonly been followed by significant improvements. As a device for rationalizing and strengthening campus library services and collections, the survey has proved itself. One might conclude that the heyday of its usefulness has passed. An examination of *Library Literature* for the past five years would seem to support that view. The number of general, broad institutional library surveys listed in the past five years is only three, or six, if groups of institutions are included. Instead of the general survey, studies or surveys of various aspects of college and university libraries are recorded. In this record one might perceive the specialized study as superseding the more inclusive approach.

But the Downs bibliography shows three large, general surveys—Utah, Purdue, and Brigham Young—in this period. In addition, there was the Canadian *Survey* as well as the surveys of library resources in several states, in all of which Downs was involved.

The evidence is thus contradictory and confusing. It seems clear that some institutions, their administrative officers, and their librarians are convinced that the general library survey is an effective instrument for the improvement of their libraries. As long as this opinion is held, it seems likely that surveys will continue to be recommended and made.

At the same time, more specific and limited studies of particular facets or problems of libraries may be expected to increase, as libraries grow in size and complexity. This is a natural, evolutionary development in the interests of economy, manageability, and expertise. But another factor may also be operative in this situation. The general institutional library survey depended for much of its effectiveness on comparisons with peer institutions and on assessments of the local situation in relation to ALA or other standards. Under some circumstances, these approaches may still be valid. In others, there is reason to believe that administrative and appropriating bodies will not be persuaded by such comparisons but, instead, will require evidence or demonstration of need in terms of formulas, performance budgets, and cost benefit evaluations. Such measures are more demanding and can probably not be adequately ascertained in the relatively short visits that have served as the basis for surveys in the past. If these types of evaluations are required, it will not be feasible at the same time to cover the spectrum from library governance to collections, facilities, and staff as was commonly done in the general survey.

If one attempts to speculate on future developments, it seems reasonable to suggest that the general university library survey may be expected to be used less frequently in the next generation than it has been since 1935; that the more specialized study may be expected more frequently; and that more sophisticated analyses and evaluations, in keeping with developing trends in university budgeting and management, may be required in order to effect the improvements which the general survey has brought to many libraries in the past thirty-five years. Perhaps a method of joining the new techniques to the well-established procedures of the survey may evolve as the most effective review instrument in the last third of the century.

About the Authors

Stephen A. McCarthy, as the Executive Secretary of the Association of Research Libraries, is probably in the best position in the library world to know what is happening in the major libraries of our country. Beginning with his landmark survey of

Cornell University Libraries in 1947, he has participated in others around the world: New Hampshire, McGill, MILC, Dalhousie, Cairo, Alexandria, Great Britain. Through his long acquaintance with Downs in Association of Research Libraries and American Libraries Association work and the mutual respect these contacts engendered, he logically writes in an area of work they shared for many years.

As one of the industrious assistants to Steve McCarthy in the Association of Research Libraries headquarters, Murray L. Howder has added a new dimension to an already notably varied record of teaching, editorial, and translating functions closely allied to librarianship. His contribution to this essay should bring a youthful view to a collection of subjects and authors almost completely of the older generation.

PUBLICATIONS OF ROBERT B. DOWNS

by Clarabelle Gunning

AMERICAN LIBRARY RESOURCES

"Special Collections for the Study of History and Literature in the Southeast" (With Louis R. Wilson). *Papers of the Bibliographical Society of America* 28:97–131. 1934.

"The State Document Center Plan in North Carolina." Chicago: ALA, *Public Documents:* 41–46. 1934.

"Southern Library Resources." *South Atlantic Bulletin* 1:1. 1935.

"Development in the South." Chicago: ALA, *Public Documents:* 32–36. 1935.

"A Proposal to Modify the System of Distribution of State Publications." Chicago: ALA, *Public Documents:* 67–68. 1935.

"Mobilization of Library Resources." *School and Society* 43:368–370. March 14, 1936.

American Library Association. "Report of Committee on Resources of Southern Libraries." Chicago: ALA, 1936. (Also in: Barker, T. D., *Librarian of the South.* Chicago: ALA, 1936. Appendix A.)

"Regional Planning of Document Collections in the South." Chicago: ALA, *Public Documents:* 162–72. 1936.

"The South Looks at Its Libraries." *Social Forces* 15:123–127. October 1936.

Review of W. S. Hoole's *Checklist and Finding List of Charleston Periodicals, 1732–1864. North Carolina Historical Review* 14:205–207. April 1937.

"The South and Its Libraries." *American Scholar* 6:245–248. Spring 1937.

"Surveying the Resources of Southern Libraries." *ALA Bulletin* 31:673–676. October 15, 1937.

Review of *A Checklist of United States Newspapers (and Weeklies before 1800) in the General Library of Duke University. North Carolina Historical Review* 15:319–320. July 1938.

Resources of Southern Libraries; a Survey of Facilities for Research. Chicago: ALA, 1938. 370 pp.

"Organization and Preservation of Manuscripts in the University of North Carolina Library." Chicago: ALA, *Public Documents:* 373–379. 1938.

Guide for the Description and Evaluation of Research Materials. Chicago: ALA, 1939. 49 pp.

Review of D. C. McMurtrie's *Eighteenth Century North Carolina Imprints, 1749–1800. North Carolina Historical Review* 16:458–460. October 1939.

"Notable Materials Added to American Libraries, 1938–1939." *Library Quarterly* 10:157–191. April 1940.

Review of *Archives and Libraries* edited by A. F. Kuhlman. *Library Quarterly* 10:285–286. April 1940.

Review of Bibliographical Planning Committee of Philadelphia's *A Faculty Survey of the University of Pennsylvania Libraries. Library Journal* 65:490. June 1, 1940.

"Resources of American Libraries; third annual report of the ALA Board on Resources of American Libraries." *ALA Bulletin* 34:540–542. September 15, 1940.

"Problems in the Acquisition of Research Materials." In: *The Acquisition and Cataloging of Books,* pp. 59–75. Chicago: University of Chicago Press, 1940.

"Notable Materials Added to American Libraries, 1939–1940." *Library Quarterly* 11:257–301. July 1941.

"Technique of the Library Resources Survey." *Special Libraries* 32:113–115, 140–141. April 1941.

Review of *Philadelphia Libraries and Their Holdings. Library Quarterly* 11:378–379. July 1941.

"The Long Island Historical Society Library." *Long Island Historical Society Quarterly* 3:4:99–102. October 1941.

"Resources of American Libraries; the fourth annual report of the ALA Board on Resources of American Libraries." *ALA Bulletin* 35:571–573. October 15, 1941.

"Notable Materials Added to American Libraries, 1940–1941." *Library Quarterly* 12:175–220. April 1942.

Editor, *Union Catalogs in the United States*. Chicago: ALA, 1942. 409 pp.

Resources of New York City Libraries. Chicago: ALA, 1942. 458 pp.

"Board on Resources of American Libraries." Fifth Annual Report. *ALA Bulletin* 36:695–697. October 15, 1942.

"The Long Island Historical Society" (With Edna Huntington). *New York History* 23:522–526. October 1942.

Preface to A. I. Katsh, ed. *The Solomon Rosenthal Collection of Hebraica*. New York. 1942.

Preface to M. M. Kaplan, ed. *Panorama of Ancient Letters; Four and a Half Centuries of Hebraica and Judaica*. New York. 1942.

"Expanding the National Union Catalog." *ALA Bulletin* 37:432–434. November 1943.

Review of John Van Male's *Resources of Pacific Northwest Libraries*. *Library Journal* 68:948–49. November 15, 1943.

Review of A. F. Kuhlman's *North Texas Regional Libraries*. *Library Quarterly* 14:254–256. July 1944.

Another review of above in: *American Archivist* 7:2:135–137. April 1944.

Review of Fremont Rider's *The Scholar and the Future of the Research Library*. *Journal of English and Germanic Philology* 44:98–100. January 1945.

Review of Philadelphia Bibliographical Center and Union Library Catalogue's "Documentation on a Regional Basis; Symposium on Post-War Activities." *Papers of the Bibliographical Society of America* 39:86–89. 1945.

Review of Fremont Rider's *The Scholar and the Future of the Research Library*. *College and Research Libraries* 6:178–179. March 1945.

Review of *Nineteenth Century Readers Guide, 1890–1899*. *Journal of English and Germanic Philology* 44:225–227. April 1945.

"Uniform Statistics for Library Holdings." *Library Quarterly* 16:63–69. January 1946.

"Where Are America's Research Resources?" *The Scientific Monthly* 62:511–516. June 1946. Reprinted in Peru and Japan.

Review of Charles E. Rush's *Library Resources of the University of North Carolina. Library Journal* 71:341–342. March 1, 1946.

"Latin American Union Catalogs." *College and Research Libraries* 7:210–213. July 1946.

"American Library Resources." *Encyclopedia Americana* 17:357 o–q. (1949 ed.)

"Problems of German Periodicals." *College and Research Libraries* 8:303–309. July 1947.

"International Exchanges." *Science* 105:417–421. April 25, 1947.

"The Library of Congress and the Future of Its Catalogue." *Journal of Documentation* 2:248–249. March 1947.

"Many Study Photographic Processes." *Library Journal* 72:1649–1652. December 1, 1947.

Foreword to Faye's *Fifteenth Century Books in the University of Illinois.* 1949.

American Library Resources; a Bibliographical Guide, 428 pp. Chicago: ALA, 1951.

Foreword to *Collection of First Editions of Milton's Works . . . an Exhibition.* 1953.

Foreword to *An Exhibition of Some Printed Geographical Works and Atlases, 1475–1675.* 1954.

"Development of Research Collections in University Libraries." In: *University of Tennessee Library Lectures,* pp. 1–15. 1954.

Foreword to *An Exhibition of Some Latin Grammars Used or Printed in England, 1471–1699.* 1955.

Review of Richard Harwell's *Research Resources in the Georgia–Florida Libraries of SIRF. Library Journal* 81:1133–1134. May 1, 1956.

"Collecting Manuscripts: By Libraries." *Library Trends* 5:337–343. January 1957.

"Libraries in Minuscule." *College and Research Libraries* 18:11–18. January 1957.

"Distribution of American Library Resources." *College and Research Libraries* 18:181–189, 235–237. May 1957.

"The Library Collection at Mid-Twentieth Century." In: *The Nature and Development of the Library Collection,* pp. 1–12. Ann Arbor, Mich.: Edwards, 1957.

"Rare Books in American State University Libraries." *The Book Collector* 6:232–243. Autumn 1957.

Preface to *The Sandburg Range; an Exhibit of Materials from Carl Sandburg's Library.* 1958.

Foreword to *The Great Debate; Lincoln vs. Douglas; An Exhibit. University of Illinois Library.* 1958.

"Are Libraries Too Big?" *The Rub-Off* 9:2–4. March–April 1958.

"Research in Problems of Resources." *Library Trends* 6:147–159. October 1957.

Foreword to *Printed Books on Architecture 1485–1805; a Brief History and a Catalog of the Exhibition.* 1960.

"Price Tag on a University Library" (With Robert F. Delzell). *College and Research Libraries* 21:359–361, 404. September 1960.

Strengthening and Improving Library Resources for Southern Higher Education. Atlanta: SREB, 1962. 23 pp.

American Library Resources; a Bibliographical Guide. Supplement, 1950–1961. Chicago: ALA, 1962. 226 pp.

Foreword to *Early Geology in the Mississippi Valley, an Exhibition.* 1962.

Resources of North Carolina Libraries. Raleigh: Governor's Commission on Library Resources, 1964. 292 pp. Revised printed ed., 236 pp. 1965.

"Special Collections in University of Illinois Library." *Illinois Libraries* 47:861–868. November 1965.

"Doctoral Programs and Library Resources." *College and Research Libraries* 27:123–129, 141. March 1966.

"Illinois' Library Resources." *Illinois History* 19:185–186. May 1966.

Resources of Missouri Libraries. Jefferson City: Missouri State Library, 1966. 190 pp.

"Government Publications in American Libraries." *Library Trends* 15:178–194. July 1966.

"Current Trends in Collection Development in University Libraries: The University of Illinois Library." *Library Trends* 15:258–265. October 1966.

"Development of Research Collections in University Libraries." In: *The Library in the University; the University of Tennessee Library Lectures, 1949–1966,* pp. 61–75. Hamden, Connecticut: Shoe String Press, 1967.

"Report re Library Study." *Proceedings Annual Meeting Association of Universities and Colleges of Canada*, pp. 57–61, 183–188, 1966.

Review of Lee Ash's *The Scope of Toronto's Central Library. Library Journal* 92:3617. October 15, 1967.

Resources of Canadian Academic and Research Libraries. Ottawa: Association of Universities and Colleges of Canada, 1967. 301 pp.

Ressources des Bibliothèques d' Université et de Recherche au Canada. Ottawa: Assoc. des Universités et Collèges du Canada, 1967. 325 pp.

Foreword to *An Exhibition of Books Presented to the University of Illinois Library by Ernest Ingold—Class of 1909*. Urbana: University of Illinois Library, 1969.

"Doctoral Degrees and Library Resources." *College and Research Libraries* 30: 417–427. September 1969.

University Library Statistics (Assisted by John W. Heussman). Washington, D.C.: Association of Research Libraries, 1969. 129 pp.

"Future Prospects of Library Acquisitions." *Library Trends* 18:412–421. January 1970.

University Library Statistics (Assisted by John W. Heussman). Chicago: ALA, 1970. 129 pp.

Unpublished Report

A Survey of Research Materials in North Carolina Libraries, 1937. 52 pp.

LIBRARY COOPERATION

"A Plan for University Library Cooperation" (With Harvie Branscomb). *School and Society* 42:64–66. July 13, 1935.

"A Venture in University Library Cooperation" (With Harvie Branscomb). *Library Journal* 60:877–879. November 15, 1935.

"One for All; an Historical Sketch of Library Cooperation." In: *Library of Tomorrow*, pp. 60–67. Chicago: ALA, 1939.

Library Specialization; Proceedings of an Informal Conference, etc. Chicago: ALA, 1941. 48 pp.

Review of *College and University Library Consolidations* by Mildred H. Lowell. *Education Abstracts* 7:263–264. December 1942.

Review of *The Bibliographical Center for Research, Rocky Mountain Region. Library Journal* 70:30. January 1, 1945.

"Library Cooperation in Review." *College and Research Libraries* 6:407–415. September 1945.

"Project for the Cooperative Acquisition of Recent Foreign Publications." *D.C. Libraries* 17:9–11. January 1946.

"Summary: Regional Library Centers Today: A Symposium." *College and Research Libraries* 8:68–69. January 1947.

Preface to *Conference on International Cultural, Educational, and Scientific Exchanges.* Chicago: ALA, 1947.

"Wartime Cooperative Acquisitions." *Library Quarterly* 19:157–165. July 1949.

"Report and Supplementary Report on the National Union Catalog and Related Matters." *Library of Congress Information Bulletin,* August 9–15, 1949. 24 pp.

"A Realistic Look at Library Cooperation." *Bibliographical Center for Research Bulletin,* no. 11. 1954.

"Library Cooperation and Specialization." In: *Problems and Prospects of the Research Library,* pp. 91–104. New Brunswick, N.J.: Scarecrow Press, 1955.

"Realistic Considerations in Library Cooperation." *Southeastern Librarian* 4:114–122, 138. Winter 1954.

"Cooperative Planning in Acquisitions." *Southeastern Librarian* 6:110–115. Fall 1956.

"Status and Plans for Regional Library Cooperation." *Southern College and Research Library Workshop Proceedings* pp. 45–48. 1958.

"University Library Cooperation. National and International." Szeged University Library, *Acta Bibliothecaria,* v. 2, pts. 2–4, pp. 31–41. 1959.

"Regional Library Centers." *Canadian Library Association Bulletin* 16:212–215. March 1960.

"Report of the Chairman of the Board of Directors." *Eleventh Annual Report of the Midwest Inter-Library Corporation and the Midwest Inter-Library Center, 1959–1960,* pp. 3–4. Chicago: The Center, 1961.

"Report on Farmington Plan Program." *College and Research Libraries* 23:143–145. March 1962.

Report on a Survey of the Libraries of the Arkansas Foundation of Associated Colleges. 1963. 44 pp.

A Survey of Cooperating Libraries for the Kansas City Regional Council for Higher Education. Kansas City, Missouri: The Council, 1964. 60 pp.

"A Cooperative Program for Kansas City Area Libraries." *Missouri Library Association Quarterly* 25:34–41. June 1964.

"Library Cooperation in Kansas City." *College and Research Libraries* 25:380–384. September 1964.

"College Library Cooperation in Arkansas." *Illinois Libraries* 47:197–202. March 1965.

Interinstitutional Cooperation: Values and Limitations. Washington: Association of American Colleges, 1968. 6 pp. (College Library Problems IV).

Unpublished Reports

Opportunities for Library Cooperation and Coordination in the Richmond Area; Report on a Survey with Recommendations, 1947. 17 pp.

A Survey of the Cooperative Library Program of the Associated Colleges of Central Kansas, 1969. 13 pp.

UNIVERSITY AND COLLEGE LIBRARY ADMINISTRATION

"How to Use the Library." *Colby College Library, Bulletin 18.* Waterville. 1930.

"College Curriculum Changes and the College Library." *Library Journal* 59:961–962. December 15, 1934. (Also in: *Southeastern Library Association Proceedings,* 1934.)

"New Avenues for University Library Extension Service." *ALA Bulletin* 30:820–822. August 1936.

Review of L. R. Wilson's *Library Trends. Social Forces* 16:145–147. October 1937.

"The Conference of Eastern College Librarians." *College and Research Libraries* 1:11–12, 39. December 1939.

"Conference of Eastern College Librarians." *College and Research Libraries* 2:190–192. March 1941.

"Recurring Problems in Cataloging Administration for University Libraries." *Catalogers and Classifiers Yearbook* 11:59–67. 1945.

"The Functions of the College Library." *Conference of Presidents of Negro Land-Grant Colleges. Proceedings,* pp. 50–58. 1944.

"The Place of College and Reference Library Service at A.L.A. Headquarters: A Symposium." *College and Research Libraries* 7:164–165. April 1946.

"Libraries, College and University." *Grolier Encyclopedia* 6:532–533. (1947 ed.)

Review of ALA *College and University Libraries and Librarianship. Journal of Higher Education* 18:112–113. February 1947.

"Departmental Libraries of the University." *Japan Library Association Library Journal* 42:4:286–289.

Issue Editor, *Library Trends,* "Current Trends in College and University Libraries," v. 1, no. 1, Introduction, pp. 3–7. 1952.

Foreword to Brough's *The Scholars Workshop,* Urbana, Ill.: University of Illinois Press, 1953.

"Problems of Bibliographical Control." *Library Trends* 2:498–508. April 1954.

"Current University and College Library Trends." *MLA Quarterly* 15: 65–71; 16:21, 23. September 1954–March 1955.

"The Library's Place in Today's University." *ALA Bulletin* 48:502–506. October 1954.

"Problems of Bibliographical Control." University of Idaho Library's *The Bookmark* 9:1:5–8. September 1956.

"University Libraries in the United States." *Journal of the Indian Library Association* 2:15–19. January 1957.

"Meeting Future Space Problems: University of Illinois Library." *College and Research Libraries* 19:17–18. January 1958.

"Improving Student Reading." *The Pioneer,* p. 3. May–June 1958.

"The Expanding University Library." *The Bookmark* (University of North Carolina Friends of the Library) 28:4–8. March 1959.

"The Spirit of Reference Service." Allerton Park Institute, *The Library as a Community Information Center,* pp. 1–11. 1959.

"Library Public Relations, University Libraries." *Illinois Libraries* 41: 519–523. September 1959.

"The Administrator Looks at Classification." Allerton Park Institute, *The Role of Classification in the Modern American Library*, pp. 1–7. 1960.

"Crisis in Our University Libraries." *College and Research Libraries* 22:7–10. January 1961.

"Some Current Aspects of College and University Library Administration." *Southeastern Librarian* 10:63–69, 104. Summer 1960.

"The Development of College and University Libraries in Illinois." *Illinois Libraries* 43:625–630. November 1961.

"Statement on Library Services Act, H.R. 11823." Hearings. pp. 92–96. Washington, D.C.: U.S. Government Printing Office, 1962.

"Library Services Act." *Illinois Libraries* 44:648–649. November 1962.

"The Implementation of Book Selection Policy in University and Research Libraries." Allerton Park Institute, *Selection and Acquisition Procedures in Medium-Sized and Large Libraries*, pp. 1–9. 1963.

Foreword to Verner Clapp's *The Future of the Research Library*. Urbana: University of Illinois Press, 1964.

"The Future of University Libraries." *Alabama Librarian* 15:5–9. April 1964.

A Study of the Libraries of the State-Supported Institutions of Higher Education in Arkansas. Little Rock: Arkansas Commission on Coordination of Higher Education Finance, 1964. 35 pp.

"The Future of University Libraries." In: *New Challenges for Auburn University*, pp. 2–4. Auburn, Alabama: Auburn University, 1964.

"University of Illinois Libraries" (With R. F. Delzell). *Illinois Libraries* 46:836–844. November 1964. (University of Illinois Library Seventh Addition)

"Statement on Higher Education Act of 1965." Hearings Before the Special Subcommittee on Education . . . on H.R. 3220. pp. 365–368, 869–870.

Survey of Library Space Needs of Colleges and Universities in Kansas. Topeka: Kansas Higher Education Facilities Commission, 1965. 34 pp.

"The Future of University Libraries." In: *Library Service Today*, edited by P. N. Paula, pp. 451–456. New York: Asia Publishing House, 1965.

"Current Problems Confronting American Research Libraries." In: *Timeless Fellowship, Annual Volume of Essays on Librarianship*, v. 2, pp. 31–38. Dharwar: Karnatak University Library Science Association, 1965.

"Library Automation and Mechanization: the Promise and the Reality." *Southeastern Librarian* 17:149–155. 1967.

Libraries in North Carolina Public Senior Colleges and Universities: Present Status and Future Needs. Raleigh: North Carolina Board of Higher Education, 1969. 42 pp.

"Report of the Library Committee, Illinois Board of Higher Education." 1969. Preliminary ed. 157 pp. Printed ed. 60 pp.

"Standards for University Libraries" (With John W. Heussman). *College and Research Libraries* 31:28–35. January 1970.

"Robert B. Downs." In: *The Librarian Speaking; Interviews with University Librarians,* edited by Guy R. Lyle, pp. 34–36. Athens: University of Georgia Press, 1970.

LIBRARY SURVEYS

Report of a Survey of the Libraries of Cornell University (With L. R. Wilson and M. F. Tauber). Ithaca: Cornell University, 1948. 202 pp.

A Survey of the Libraries of the University of Utah. Salt Lake City: University of Utah Libraries, 1965. 133 pp.

"Methodology of a State Library Survey." *Southeastern Librarian* 16:91–97. Summer 1966.

"Missouri Library Survey Report: Introduction and Summary." *Missouri Library Association Quarterly* 27:18–36. March 1966.

A Survey of the Libraries of the University of Georgia. Athens: University of Georgia Libraries, 1966. 93 pp.

A Survey of the Libraries of Purdue University. Lafayette: Purdue University Libraries, 1967. 169 pp.

"Survey of Purdue University Libraries." *Indiana Slant* (Indiana Chapter SLA) 30:5–6. March 1968.

Review of Maurice F. Tauber's *Library Surveys. College and Research Libraries* 29:160–162. March 1968.

A Survey of the Library of Brigham Young University. Provo: Brigham Young University Library, 1969. 165 pp.

Unpublished Reports

Report on a Survey of the Library Company of Philadelphia, 1940. 9 pp.

The Library Building Situation at Louisiana State University; a Survey Report, with Recommendations, 1947. 5 pp.

Report on a Survey of Southern Illinois University Libraries, 1960. 21 pp. (With Maurice F. Tauber.)

Comments on University of Louisville Library, 1964. 5 pp.

Location of Proposed Undergraduate Library Building, University of Wisconsin, 1965. 4 pp.

Indiana State College Library; a Brief Survey of its Book Collections, 1961. 32 pp.

Nebraska State Teachers College Library; Report on Building Plans and General Development, Chadron, 1962. 6 pp.

Kearney State College Library; Recommendations for the Development of Its Book Collections, 1963. 23 pp.

Nebraska State Teachers College Library, Kearney—Building Plans; Recommendations and Suggestions, 1961. 7 pp.

University of Puerto Rico Libraries; Report on a Brief Survey, 1964. 13 pp.

Library of Kansas State College of Pittsburg; Report of a Survey, 1963. 26 pp.

Notes on a Brief Survey of the Fisk University Library, 1965. 10 pp.

Report on Survey of Peru (Nebraska) *State College Library, 1966.* 29 pp.

Survey of University of Cincinnati Libraries, 1968. 31 pp. (With Robert L. Talmadge.)

A Survey of Northern Illinois University's Library Space Needs. 9 pp. (With Lucien W. White.)

Report on the Place of Departmental Libraries at Georgia Institute of Technology, 1968. 5 pp.

Report on a Brief Survey of the Southwestern State College Library, Weatherford, Oklahoma, 1969. 20 pp. (With Edward G. Holley.)

Slippery Rock State College Library. Report on a Brief Survey. 1969. 29 pp.

Program for the Development of the Governors State University Library, 1970. 16 pp.

Virginia's College and University Libraries; Report of a Survey. Richmond: State Council of Higher Education for Virginia, 1970. Prelim. ed. 79 pp.

LIBRARY PERSONNEL AND EDUCATION

Review of E. J. Reece's *Programs for Library Schools. Journal of Higher Education* 15:497–498. December 1944.

"Preparation for Librarianship." *Illinois Libraries* 26:1:5–10. January 1944.

"Academic Status for University Librarians: A New Approach." *College and Research Libraries* 7:6–9, 26. January 1946.

"Preparation of Specialists for University Libraries." *Special Libraries* 37:209–213. September 1946.

Review of Joseph L. Wheeler's *Programs and Problems in Education for Librarianship. Journal of Higher Education* 17:447–448. November 1946.

Review of J. Periam Danton's *Education for Librarianship. Journal of Higher Education* 18:334–335. June 1947.

Foreword (With Kenneth Shaffer) to Lancour's *Issues in Library Education.* Ann Arbor, Mich.: Edwards, 1949.

Review of Berelson's *Education for Librarianship. Journal of Higher Education* 22:164–165. March 1951.

"Are College and University Librarians Academic?" *College and Research Libraries* 15:9–14. January 1954.

"Education for Librarianship: The SWLA Education Panel." *SWLA Papers and Proceedings,* pp. 57–62. 1952.

"The Successful Supervisor." In: *The School Library Supervisor,* pp. 72–78. Chicago: ALA, 1956.

"The Current Status of University Library Staffs." *College and Research Libraries* 18:375–385. September 1957.

"Education for Librarianship at Illinois." *Illinois Libraries* 40:186–189. March 1958.

"The Art of Supervision." *Oklahoma Librarian* 8:84, 98–103. October 1958.

Editor, *The Status of American College and University Librarians.* Chicago: ALA, 1958. 176 pp.

"The Art of Supervision." *North Carolina Libraries* 17:75–80. Spring 1959.

"The Place of Librarians in Colleges and Universities." *North Carolina Libraries* 18:34–41. Winter 1960.

"Is Librarianship a Profession?" *Kentucky Library Association Bulletin* 24:14–18. January 1960.

"Education and the Recruitment of Law Librarians." *Law Library Journal* 55:204–208. August 1962.

"The Age of the Egghead." *The Rub-Off* 14:2–5. January–February 1963.

"¿Es la Bibliotecología una Profesión?" *Boletin de la Sociedad de Bibliotecarios de Puerto Rico* 1:16–20. 1962.

"Resources for Research in Librarianship." *Library Trends* 13:6–14. July 1964.

"Status of University Librarians—1964." *College and Research Libraries* 25:253–258. July 1964.

"Professional Duties in University Libraries" (With Robert F. Delzell). *College and Research Libraries* 26:30–39, 69. January 1965.

"Opportunities for Librarians in the Humanities and Fine Arts." *Proceedings of the Canadian Library Association, 21st Annual Conference,* pp. 23–28. Calgary, Canada, 1966.

"Aspects of Library Personnel." *Southeastern Librarian* 16:150–157. Fall 1966.

"Quarters and Facilities: Administrator's Point of View." *Journal of Education for Librarianship* 7:84–89. Fall 1966.

"The Place of College Librarians in the Academic World." *California Librarian* 28:101–106. April 1967.

"Aspects of Library Personnel." *Timeless Fellowship,* Dharwar, India: Karnatak University Library Science Association, 1966–1967. pp. 3–4: 1–14.

"Education for Librarianship in the United States and Canada." In: *Library Education: an International Survey,* edited by L. E. Bone, pp. 1–20. Urbana: University of Illinois Graduate School of Library Science, 1968.

"Status of Academic Librarians in Retrospect." *College and Research Libraries* 29:253–258. July 1968.

"The School's Third Quarter Century." In: *Reminiscences: Seventy-five Years of a Library School,* edited by Barbara Olsen Slanker, pp. 89–

93. Urbana: University of Illinois Graduate School of Library Science, 1969. pp. 89–93.

"Status of California State College Librarians." *American Libraries* 1:57–59. January 1970.

Unpublished Reports

Professional Personnel Procedures in the City University of New York Libraries, 1965. 22 pp.

Report on the Department of Library Science, University of Michigan, 1967. 15 pp. (With Lester Asheim, L. Quincy Mumford, and Raynard Swank.)

LIBRARIES AND LIBRARY EDUCATION ABROAD

"Japan's New National Library." *College and Research Libraries* 10:381–387, 416. October 1949.

National Diet Library: Report on Technical Processes, Bibliographical Services, and General Organization. Tokyo: National Diet Library, 1948. 60 pp.

"Libraries in Japan, 1948." *ILA Record* 2:2:8–11. December 1948.

"Japan's New Library School." In: Jt. Comm. of the Far Eastern Assoc. and the ALA, *Oriental Collections, USA and Abroad,* pp. 12–21. Ames, 1951.

"Mission in Mexico." *ALA Bulletin* 46:328–329, 349–350. November 1952.

"Problems and Prospects of the National University Libraries of Mexico." *SWLA Papers and Proceedings* 31–43. 1952.

"The Joint Meeting of SWLA-Mexican Libraries." *SWLA Papers and Proceedings,* 5–9. 1952.

"Librarianship in Turkey." *Stechert–Hafner Book News* 10:17–18. October 1955.

"Observaciones y Sugestiones Sobre la Organización de las Bibliotecas de la Universidad de México." *Boletín de la Biblioteca Nacional de México* 3–16. July–September 1952.

"Librarianship in Japan, Mexico, and Turkey." *ILA Record* 10:1:5–9, 16–17. July 1956. Excerpts in MSU *Friends of the Library News* 12:2:4–7. 1957.

"How to Start a Library School." *ALA Bulletin* 52:399–405. June 1958.

"How to Start a Library School," tr. by Soo Young Cho. *Korean Library Bulletin* 7:8:33–45. 1958 (in Korean).

"Libraries—Modern Foreign Libraries—Japan." *Encyclopedia Americana* 17:375. 1960.

"One Hundred Notable Libraries of the World." *Encyclopedia Americana* 17:421–432. 1962.

The Kabul University Library; an Evaluation of its Present Status and Recommendations for its Future Growth and Development. Kabul: Afghanistan, USAID, 1963. 60 pp.

"One Hundred Notable Libraries of the World." *AB Bookman's Yearbook, 1964,* pp. 6–16. Newark, New Jersey: Antiquarian Bookman, 1964.

"Library Problems of Emerging Nations." *Law Library Journal* 57:377–382. November 1964.

Foreword to Lester Asheim's *Librarianship in Developing Countries,* pp. v–vii. Urbana: University of Illinois Press, 1966.

Unpublished Reports

Observations and Suggestions on Organization of National University of Mexico Libraries, 1952. 13 pp.

Summary Report on Institute of Librarianship, University of Ankara, 1955. 4 pp.

Report on a Visit to the Escuela Interamericana de Bibliotecologia (Medellín, Colombia). 7 pp. (With Herbert Goldhor.)

Mission to Brazil; Report to USIA Advisory Committee on Cultural Information, March 10, 1961. 5 pp.

Report to the Agency for International Development on Programs of Library Development at the Middle East Technical University and Hacettepe University, Ankara, Turkey, 1968. 18 pp.

INTELLECTUAL FREEDOM

"Some Current Delusions, or Horsefeathers in Librarianship." *Southeastern Librarian* 3:1:20–27. Spring 1953.

Robert S. Allen Reports. (Column published September 14, 1953, released by Post-Hall Syndicate.)

"Some Current Delusions." In: Marshall's *Books, Libraries, Librarians,* pp. 312–323. 1955.

"Liberty and Justice in Books." *ALA Bulletin* 51:407–410. June 1957.

"Censorship." *American Library Annual and Book Trade Almanac, 1959,* pp. 91–92. New York: R. R. Bowker, 1958.

"The Book Burners Cannot Win." In: *The First Freedom,* pp. 210–212. Chicago: ALA, 1960.

Editor, *The First Freedom.* Chicago: ALA, 1960. 469 pp.

"Foreword" to Dan Lacy's *Freedom and Communications.* Urbana: University of Illinois Press, 1961.

"Apologist for Censorship." *Library Journal* 86:2042–2044. June 1, 1961.

"Censorship Debate: Between Two Stools." *Library Journal* 86:2580–2582. August 1961.

"Book Banning vs. the Right to Read." *Kansas Business Review* 15:2–4. March 1962.

"Story Without an Ending: review of *Versions of Censorship,*" ed. by John McCormick and Mairi MacInnes. *Library Journal* 87:1766–1767. May 1, 1962.

"University Faculty and Students Thrive on Controversy." *Library Journal* 87:2304, 2353. June 15, 1962.

"Communist Propaganda." *Library Journal* 87:2506–2507. July 1962.

"Book Banning vs. the Right to Read." *The College Store Journal* 29:100–104. August–September 1962.

"Trustees and Intellectual Freedom." *Illinois Libraries* 45:256–259. May 1963.

"Freedom to Read." *Wyoming Library Roundup* June 1966, pp. 26–32.

Foreword to Ralph E. McCoy's *Freedom of the Press; an Annotated Bibliography,* pp. vii–xi. Carbondale: Southern Illinois University Library, 1968.

"Apologist for Censorship." In: *Book Selection and Censorship in the Sixties,* edited by Eric Moon, pp. 251–254. New York: R. R. Bowker, 1969.

"Censorship Debate: Between Two Stools." Ibid. pp. 256–258.

"Intellectual Freedom: the American Tradition." *Library Trends* 19:8–18. July 1970.

INFLUENCE OF BOOKS

"The Story of Books." *University of North Carolina Library Extension Publication* 1:6. 1935. 42 pp.

"The Game of Book Collecting." *Carolina Magazine*, 26–28. March 1937.

"Books on the War Fronts." *Illinois Libraries* 26:3:105–108. March 1944.

Review of Sidney Ditzion's *Arsenal of a Democratic Culture. Annals of the American Academy of Political and Social Science* 254:176–177. November 1947.

Foreword to Ridenour–Shaw–Hill's *Bibliography in an Age of Science.* 1951.

Foreword of Guinzburg–Fraze–Waller's *Books and the Mass Market.* 1953.

"Are Books Obsolete?" *Library Journal* 79:2269–2273. December 1, 1954.

Foreword to *Three Presidents and Their Books.* 1955.

"Les Quinze Livres Exerçant une Influence Capitale Sur la Vie des Nations." *Bulletin de l'Association des Bibliothécaires Turcs.* 3:144–162. 1955.

"Books That Changed the World; an Introduction." *ALA Bulletin* 50:29–33. Jauary 1956.

Books That Changed the World. New York: New American Library of World Literature; Chicago: American Library Association, 1956. 200 pp.

"Books That Changed the World." *The Bookmark* 9:98–101. June 1957.

Books That Changed the World. Tokyo: Arechi Shuppansha, 1957. 242 pp. (in Japanese).

"Books Are Here to Stay." *ALA Bulletin* 51:665–672. October 1957.

Review of *American Panorama*, edited by Eric Larrabee. *Library Quarterly* 28:78. January 1958.

"From Cicero to Cerf." *Wilson Library Bulletin* 32:479–482. March 1958.

The Power of Books. Syracuse, New York: Syracuse University Press, 1958. 23 pp.

"The Influence of Books." *Ankara Üniversitesi Dil ve Tarih-Cografya Fakültesi Dergisi* 13:3:1–16.

Books That Changed the World. Tehran, Iran: Ebne Sina, 1958. 320 pp. (in Persian).

Books That Changed the World. Seoul: Chongum Sa (Jung-Eun Sa), 1959. 347 pp. (in Korean).

Buku-Buku Jang Merobah Dunia (Books That Changed the World). Djakarta: P. T. Pembangunan, 1959. 212 pp. (in Indonesian).

"Books in the Twentieth Century." In: *Of, By, and For Librarians,* edited by J. D. Marshall, pp. 26–41. Hamden, Connecticut: Shoe String Press, 1960.

"Sixteen Books That Changed the World." *The Rotarian* 97:12–15. September 1960.

Afterword. In: Upton Sinclair's *The Jungle.* New York: New American Library, 1960. pp. 343–350. Signet ed.

"Classics in Science." Allerton Park Institute, *Collecting Science Literature for General Reading,* 1961. pp. 1–22.

Molders of the Modern Mind. New York: Barnes & Noble, 1961. 396 pp. (cloth and paperback eds.).

Books That Changed the World. Dacca, East Pakistan: Asia Book House, 1960. 230 pp. (in Bengali).

"Molders of the Modern Mind—Efficiency Expert." F. W. Taylor's *Principles of Scientific Management. The Executive* 5:3–4. December 1961.

Libros que Han Cambiado el Mundo (Books That Changed the World). Madrid: Aguilar, 1961. 306 pp. (in Spanish).

Books That Changed the World. Lahore: Sh: Ghulam Ali & Sons, 1961. 312 pp. (in Urdu).

Kutub Ghayyarat Wagh al Alam (Books That Changed the World), translated by Ahmad Sadeq Hamdi. Cairo: Anglo, March 1958. 383 pp. (in Arabic).

Books That Changed the World. Tokyo: Arechi Shuppansha, 1963. 250 pp. 2d ed. (in Japanese).

"The Power of Books." Special Supplement to *J. Walter Thompson Company News* 19:14:51–54. April 10, 1964.

Famous Books, Ancient and Medieval. New York: Barnes & Noble, 1964. 329 pp.

"Power of Books." *Forum of Phi Eta Sigma* 35:1–6, 13–15. 1965.

Buku-Buku Yang Merobah Dunia (Books That Changed the World). Kuala Lumpur: Sharikat Berhad Penerbitan dan Perdagangan Malaysia, 1964. 267 pp. (in Malayan).

Famous Books Since 1492. New York: Barnes & Noble, 1965. 396 pp. (Originally published as *Molders of the Modern Mind.*)

"Books That Changed the World." *Oklahoma Librarian* 16:32–43. April 1966.

"The Publications Explosion." *Library Binder* 14:3–4. May 1966.

"The Publications Explosion." *Wyoming Library Roundup,* June 1966. p. 33–41.

Books That Changed the World. Taipei, Taiwan: Pure Literature Monthly Company, 1968. 313 pp. (in Chinese).

Books That Changed the World. Saigon: Van Dan, 1968. 406 pp. (in Vietnamese).

Books That Changed the World. Tokyo, 1968. 3d ed. (in Japanese).

Molders of the Modern Mind. Lahore, Pakistan: Shaikh Gulam Ali, 1968. 548, 16 pp. (in Urdu).

Books That Changed America. Denver: University of Denver, Graduate School of Librarianship, 1969. 10 pp.

Books That Changed America. New York: Macmillan, 1970. 280 pp.

AMERICAN HUMOR AND FOLKLORE

"American Humor" (With Elizabeth C. Downs). *University of North Carolina Library Extension Publication* 4:2. 1937. 45 pp.

American Humorous Folklore. Minneapolis: University of Minnesota Press, 1950. 42 pp.

The Family Saga and Other Phases of American Folklore (With Mody C. Boatright and John T. Flanagan). Urbana: University of Illinois Press, 1958. 65 pp.

The Bear Went Over the Mountain; Tall Tales of American Animals. New York: Macmillan, 1964. 358 pp.

GENERAL

"A Spanish Literary Index." *Library Journal* 53:1050. December 15, 1928.

Review of E. W. Knight and Agatha B. Boyd's *The Graduate School Research and Publications. Library Quarterly* 18:75–76. January 1948.

Foreword to John T. Winterich's *Three Lantern Slides.* 1949.

"No Book Should Be Out of Reach." *California Librarian* 13:77–80, 110–111. December 1951.

Foreword to Ray–Weber–Carter's *Nineteenth Century English Books.* 1952.

"One Library World." *ALA Bulletin* 46:215–217. July–August 1952.

"The ALA Today. A 1953 Stocktaking Report." *ALA Bulletin* 47:397–399. October 1953.

"Books and Libraries in the USA." *North Carolina Libraries* 13:49–52, 65. January 1955.

"President's Message." *ILA Record* 9:3:35–36. January 1956.

"Problems of Bibliographical Control." University of Idaho Library's *The Bookmark* 9:1:5–8. September 1956.

Review of Louis R. Wilson's *The University of North Carolina, 1900–1930. College and Research Libraries* 18:419–420. September 1957.

"Do Libraries Have a Future?" *Maryland Libraries* 24:79–85. Summer 1958.

"We and the ALA." *Wilson Library Bulletin* 34:668–670. May 1960.

"University's Observance of Land-Grant Centennial." University of Illinois *Faculty Letter*, no. 23, October 31, 1961. 4 pp.

"Little Libraries Can Be Big." *The Rotarian* 102:28–31. March 1963. Reprinted in the *Congressional Record*, November 22, 1963.

"The Small Library: Decline and Fall." *Wilson Library Bulletin* 37:772–774. May 1963.

"The Influence of Librarians on Book Publishing." In: *Librarianship and Publishing*, edited by Carl H. Melinat, pp. 7–18. Syracuse, N.Y.: School of Library Science, Syracuse University, 1963.

Review of Louis R. Wilson's *The University of North Carolina Under Consolidation, 1931–1963: History and Appraisal. Library Quarterly* 34:400–401. October 1964.

How To Do Library Research. Urbana: University of Illinois Press, 1966. 179 pp.

Editor (With Frances B. Jenkins), "Bibliography: Current State and Future Trends." *Library Trends* 15:335–919. January–April 1967.

Review of Louis R. Wilson's *Education and Libraries; Selected Papers*, edited by Maurice F. Tauber and Jerrold Orne. *Southeastern Librarian* 17:34–36. Spring 1967.

Bibliography: Current State and Future Trends (With Frances B. Jenkins). Urbana: University of Illinois Press, 1967. 611 pp.

"Foreword" to Erik Dal's *Scandinavian Bookmaking in the Twentieth Century*. Copenhagen: Christian Ejlers' Forlag, 1968. pp. 9–10.

About the Author

Mrs. Clarabelle Gunning began her life-long career in the University of Illinois Library in 1938, five years before Downs came in 1943. From that small function as a clerk-stenographer in the librarian's office, she moved quietly into his professional life as a dedicated compiler, editor, tracker, and mover to assure the unending flow of his writing and professional activity into the stream of library literature. Unofficial but authentic bibliographer, one of the quiet forces behind a great man, Mrs. Gunning devoted virtually all of her working years to Downs and Illinois.

Date Due